True intimacy...

On a rainy day, in the rainforest outside of Bogota, Colombia, I arrived in the small farming community of Sylvania. We held a meeting to share The Great Circle of Desire. A dozen folks showed up, 3 couples, and many curious singles.

The house was built on the side of a mountain from materials in the immediate jungle. An open air home, it allowed the humid breeze to flow through. Let's just say, it was not what I am used to, but the feeling of community was so beautiful I was able to enjoy it.

I asked for a couple to demonstrate in front of the group. Maia and Juan looked at each other, and nodded.

They were a "happy enough" couple, together for 5 years, but they had come to the meeting to learn how to be closer. He stood, tall and strong, then taking her hand, he led her to the front of the room.

Easily a foot taller than her, he rested his chin on top of her head as she entered his embrace. His arms engulfed her slight frame. I guided them into The Power Embrace.

As she nestled her cheek into his chest, I adjusted their hands on each other and they found a comfortable position. The whole group was silent, watching, waiting for this magic to happen.

I felt the energy between them easily, getting a few goosebumps as I felt them connect. Maia had closed her eyes, her dark hair framed her relaxed face. She was already smiling.

Juan took a deep breath, and as he let it out with a soothing sigh, the room shifted. Everyone seemed to feel it. Maia inhaled, almost a gasp, as waves of love became palpable in the room. My body was covered in goosebumps, and I knew it was working.

For the first time in five years of marriage, Juan felt his wife's heart flowing love into him. He was overwhelmed, and pulled her even closer.

The couple remained perfectly still and quiet. We watched them, together, in respectful silence, and they began rocking slowly.

She was completely relaxed, sighing softly in his embrace. Love flowed between them, and then around the room. I watched the others soften, tears spilling with awe as they too felt the love flowing. The embrace lasted several minutes more, and nobody made a sound. Juan could not find words for what his heart had felt with his own wife. It changed their lives forever...

A Private Moment...

After one of my meetups, a young woman came to me privately.

Out of frustration, Ann had completely given up on having a sex life. Since she had been married, life was busy. Though she and her husband had been married only 2 years, they both worked full time, and were always tired. Their sex life had died.

She had just watched people successfully practicing The Great Circle of Desire, but her husband wasn't with her that evening so she felt frustrated.

She expressed her anger and sadness, "I'm only 29 and I don't feel like a woman anymore! I don't care about having sex for the rest of my life. My husband is loving, but I feel like I'm way too masculine, and we are out of balance."

Too many husbands have experienced when their wives give up sex completely, but they have no idea why it happens.

I asked if she thought her husband would be open to learning the practice, and she eagerly nodded.

"Yes! He wants this fixed as much as I do, but we don't know where to start!"

We set up a private session in their home. When I met her husband, I understood. He was a big, warm, teddy bear of a man, but he didn't seem confident with her.

I instructed Ann to let him hold her, which took a minute. She hadn't relaxed in so long!

As we went through the practice, making adjustments and working through some deep breathing, they both began to flow. I coached him on allowing his energy to flow from his genitals into her, and I instructed her to allow it to flow up and out of her heart and back into him.

He wasn't quite getting it, and I felt her begin to tense up, so I asked him to make some sound when he exhaled. He did. She felt it. As he groaned, low and deep, she received his primal, masculine energy for the first time and let out a deep moan. Her body relaxed. There it was. The connection had been made.

He held her in his arms, and told her how beautiful she was. As the energy increased, the spark between them was reignited. They both began to make more noise, and she swayed in his arms in pleasure.

I knew they would want time alone, so I quietly excused myself, feeling the full body goosebumps again.

What a gift to help people feel this ! I heard back from Ann a few days later. She sounded alive again, and wanted to let me know her husband said "THANK YOU" for saving our marriage!

Polarity...

As I shared The Great Circle of Desire, I realized that my meetups attracted couples who were heterosexual and had lost the spark in their relationship.

I pondered the sex lives of people of other gender identities and relationship preferences, and began to explore the polarity, and giver-receiver roles more deeply.

I mean, The Great Circle of Desire would still work, right?

I called my friend, Sarah, who had been married to Erica for several years. After sharing my question about same sex couples using the polarity of The Great Circle of Desire, she volunteered to try it with her partner, and invited me over to coach them.

When I arrived, they were ready and waiting.

Sarah was a feisty, curvy, wild woman, with bright red hair, and Irish green eyes. She pulled me into a hug right after opening the door. Over her shoulder, Erica smiled as she approached, her bright blue eyes sparkled behind black framed glasses that matched her spiky hair. She came up behind Sarah, wrapping her arms around both of us and we all busted up laughing.

I have always been very open and affectionate with people in general, but my relationships had always been with men. I was eager to see The Great Circle of Desire at work between two women.

We discussed who would be the giver and receiver, and it took very little instruction before they melted into a perfect Power Embrace! Erica acted as giver and held Sarah, just like Juan had held Maia.

Sarah relaxed into Erica's arms, their body type was similar, and they fit together well. Erica was visibly stronger, as if she worked out a lot, and I watched her more masculine mannerisms as she held Sarah.

Goosebumps covered my body once again as love flowed between them. It was so simple. This practice transcended gender and sexual preference!

After several minutes, they ended the embrace, both looking a little blissed out, smiling.

I had the thought to ask them to switch roles, and they were all about it! Sarah held Erica that time, allowing the energy to move the other way.

My eyes filled with tears as I saw love flowing so perfectly and naturally.

Even though Erica was usually the giver she was able to relax into Sarah's arms, surrender, and receive.

They were surprised at how easy it was to switch roles, and how recharged they both felt after the embraces.

I thanked them and left, my heart bursting open with the thought of sharing this with the world...

Cosmic Kari Stars

The Great Circle of Desire

COSMIC KARI STARS

THE GREAT CIRCLE OF DESIRE

By Cosmic Kari Star

Published by Flowganize, llc UNITED STATES

Cover Design Book Design and Content Editing by Andrea Nicole King

Original Cover Artwork ©George Atherton

Paperback ISBN: 978-1-7329271-1-7
Digital ISBN: 978-1-732971-0-0

Disclaimer:

Please be advised of the following: The information contained in this book, on any related social media, and resulting communications is educational in nature. It is provided only as general information, and should not be taken as medical or psychological advice. Transmission of the information presented is not intended to create a client practitioner relationship between Cosmic Kari Star or any of her associates. These teachings should not be relied upon as coaching, spiritual medical, psychological or other professional advice of any kind. Please seek professional counsel if needed. Stories are examples with names changed from actual experiences.

Dedication and Acknowledgements

This book is dedicated to you, the one reading it. If you are brave enough to pick it up, read it, and put these concepts into practice, you will have access to the incredibly intimate connections with people in your life, and the BEST SEX EVER!

And now, to acknowledge some of the amazing people who have been my support and cheerleaders...

Mamie, childhood friends since 5th grade and my bff, had created the name with me of THE CIRCLE OF DESIRE. The day came when she said, "You must stop everything now and write this book! It's important! Make it short, to-the-point. It must be written." She knew many couples who were suffering and how much they needed this. Now a trainer of CEO's, she has an intuitive knowing and vast perspective backed by solid spot-on rationality.

Andrea, my editor, and a dear friend, helped me add the "Great" to the title. I loved the significance it added, which I felt was truly deserved by the importance of this information. She is the one standing by my side with her manifestation know-how, editing savvy, creative input and wisdom. I need her saying, "Yes, this is good". She has made this process remarkably easy and flow-y. A God-send. This work is a product of her love and passion, too. Wow, am I GRATEFUL!

Cassandra, my psychic coach, for being there and encouraging me through thick and thin, believing in me hundreds of times when I did not believe in myself. When I thought I couldn't do it, or was overwhelmed a bit too much, I turned to her. I finally did it, Cassandra!

Janet, my sister, has encouraged me and been the straight talker, giving me great solid support throughout my journey as a writer and we have become closer than I ever thought possible. She is a power house and I credit her as my foundation, along with my mother, Joanie. Mom has been there with loving care always, showing me what it means to be a great mom.

Claiming to be my biggest fan, I thank Stephen. Being somewhat of a hold-out on heart connection, he took the stories about disconnected sex very seriously. I was surprised it got through to him, and this encouraged me even more about the timeliness of this work. Men are ready to hear the truth, and both men and women need to show the way for each other. I APPRECIATE YOU Stephen!

To all those that have loved and supported my work and those that have blessed me with kindnesses large and small along my path, thank you! I am finally beginning the work I committed to doing as a teenager, to bring books, coaching, and teachings about the return of ecstasy to the world.

Table of Contents

Foreword
by Andrea Nicole King

I met Kari in 2009, when my life was going... okay. I wasn't unhappy, just... looking for something, but had no idea what. There was a nagging feeling that something was missing.

I was married to a wonderful man, but somehow felt like our journey together was shifting. I intuitively knew it wasn't his "fault" but spent a lot of time examining what the thing was that I was missing. I wanted to "save" the marriage.

I searched local meetups and found one called "Celebrate Sensuality". My initial reaction was intrigued yet... nervous. Like most people, I equated sensuality with sexuality, and talking about that with strangers felt very scary. It almost kept me from clicking the link to read about the group. Almost.

I felt a nudge to do it, and clicked the description and read about how the group was created for women who wanted something more in their life but didn't know what it was.

Whoa.

I broke through an irrational fear and responded "yes" to the next event, a women's group meeting. What was weird was how nervous I felt driving to it. What was even weirder was when I got there, I discovered I was not alone.

Kari opened the door with a huge smile and asked if I'd like a hug. She engulfed me warmly, and welcomed me into her home. Wow! The room was cozy, and Kari had put out a bunch of beautiful treats to nibble. Candles burned and soft music played. I felt at ease immediately.

I sat on a cozy couch as the rest of the women arrived. There were about 10 women in their 30s to 50s who all had a common thread. We all wanted to live more authentically, feel more deeply, experience life more fully. Of course this included having a more satisfying sex life, but it was so much more than that.

I cried in front of strangers for the first time in my life, actually allowing these ladies to see me, and hold a space for me to *feel something*. I was safe. I was okay. They weren't strangers, they were just like me.

We all shared our stories, finding common themes of suppression and guilt around expressing our sensual nature. We wanted to flow, and be free to explore sexually, but had held back in fear of being seen as too "slutty" or something.

We began to open up and talk about EVERYTHING!

Many of us cried, and laughed and hugged each other. It was so refreshing and freeing to feel okay, and be seen even though I felt like a hot mess.

I felt truly safe for the first time in my life, with women I didn't even really know.

Kari and I quickly became close friends, and before long, she asked me to help facilitate the meetup group. We realized that the women's group was nice, but felt we really needed to invite the men to join us.

We fumbled through, teaching, learning, and creating a space for people to connect and share in a world that shunned sensuality. We devoted our group to honoring sensuality and sexuality as sacred, and beautiful, and attracted people who desired the same thing.

It was awkward, and we laughed through it.

The best part was seeing people have those breakthroughs and find their own power and freedom. We held space for vulnerability, connection, and appreciation. We practiced it, and shared it.

During that time, Kari was teaching The Great Circle of Desire, she just hadn't yet called it that. After learning how to feel the subtle energies between two people, I found a flow of love and beautiful energy with almost everyone I tried it with.

Through our time hosting the group, Kari gave me permission to allow myself to explore who I was. She was the first one ever to tell me that it was okay to try new things, explore, and experiment.

I met people who were safe to share with and explored parts of myself I didn't know existed.

I found my voice, I found my boundaries, I found my power. It was uncomfortable, beautiful, amazing, and perfect. To this day I credit her as my first catalyst on my path of self discovery.

Cosmic Kari Star, as we call her now, has invited me to craft her 10 years of writing into books to share with the world. If you've ever talked to her, you know she is passionate about sharing her experiences and helping people connect to their own freedom, and each other.

I am honored to help her light the way with this book, this practice, and those following. We share a deep desire to help people discover their true sensual nature and live lives of freedom, ecstasy and bliss. In this technologically focused world, where we can so easily feel disconnected and alone, we are using the resources to connect instead of disconnect. A global human family is out there, who thinks like you do, and honors your sacred design.

We know that through publishing books, and using technology, we can reach out and touch so many people. Our invitation to you is to connect with us and find your tribe.

Please join us in the Facebook Group, The Great Circle of Desire, an open, yet private space to explore and share your experiences. We suspect you will meet others on a similar path of discovery, just as I did when I originally met Kari.

May you be blessed with the highest joy your heart desires, the innocence and playfulness of your inner child, the beauty of your highest truth, the depths of your sensual nature in full expression, and all of the incredible pleasure you are entitled to as a human being. With gratitude and respect for this work… let's do this.

Divine couple V, 100x120 cm, oil on canvas, by Ines Honfi

Introduction

Hi, It's Cosmic Kari! Before you read this book, I'm going to give it all away right here in the introduction. Just two little words.

Appreciation and Connection

These words may sound cliche, as they have been the subject of many self-help programs for the past decade or two. It's taken me a lot of years to understand their application to the deep dark secret of profound intimacy and amazing sex.

While those two little words seem simple, they are the keys to unlocking real human intimacy and vulnerability which creates the fertile erotic space necessary for the very best sex.

There, now you have it. If you understand it, you can put this book down and go back to your life and create the relationships you have always wanted with appreciation and connection.

Or.

If you aren't quite sure what I mean, go ahead and keep reading.

Oh! You're still here, okay, wonderful! Thank you for giving me the space to share some things with you.

When I share my discoveries, I am always met with an overwhelming request to get the word out in a BIG WAY.

To this day, it amuses me when people have their "aha" moment.

They often hit themselves on the head saying "Why didn't I know this before?"

I'm ready now to allow my discoveries to change the world and set people free. What is mind blowing to me is HOW SIMPLE IT IS!

Yes, I believe we all have ideas that we know would change the world, and this is mine.

I have been writing about my own experiences in awakening my sensuality and sexuality for over 10 years. Writing has helped me understand the value of my journey.

I have learned to accept my overweight body, and discover the heights of ecstasy I am capable of reaching. Now, my deepest desire is to share my stories and experiences with others in the hope that they too can reach this level of freedom.

In this day and age, sexuality is STILL limited and suppressed. Why do people still believe the BIG LIE that sex is bad, evil, or dirty? Why do we not talk about it openly? Why are we too shy to say words like *penis or vagina or orgasm*?

And, why does most open sex talk seem to lead to more fantasy and kink but leave partners lacking the vulnaribility and closeness they desire?

Do you want to know, really?

Good, because I have made a commitment to end The Big Lie.

What I know is that to do this, the information must have these qualities:

- ❖ It must be simple
- ❖ It must be described so anyone can feel it
- ❖ It must feel natural and balanced
- ❖ It must fulfill a need that is often missing
- ❖ It must be strong enough to transform lives immediately
- ❖ It must be gentle enough to shift people away from the spell, that sex is evil

❖ It must be presented so a new paradigm of wholesome sexuality can result

Could there be such a thing with this much power?

Yes.

Is this new information?

No.

It IS a new way to see something so simple and beautiful it's been right in front of us the whole time. Our job is to open into it, gently, and allow it to have its way with us!

I hope you find it as life-changing as it has been for so many.

That being said...
We humans seem to be suffering from more disconnection than ever, settling for sex that is far inferior to what we truly desire. Even when coupled, partners are often left wanting more.

In the studies I have done over the past 10 years, these are the most common problems which block intimacy:

❖ Honeymoon period ends and connection is lost
❖ Pornography and quick release replace intimacy
❖ Disconnected sex leaves one or both feeling empty or used
❖ Physical limitations, poor health, body or age issues
❖ Lack of boundaries, or self awareness
❖ Lack of confidence to speak up
❖ One or both resist therapy or coaching

It seems the times we live in are plagued with these issues and now more than ever, people are desperate to resolve it once and for all. Since I struggled with the same issues, I was determined to find an answer. I'm happy to tell you, I believe I've solved the problem!

This simple practice can continually bring greater fulfillment throughout your life.

It will work for you whether you are single or partnered. Although my work is based on heterosexuality, it is important for each and every one of us, regardless of orientation or status to have their needs met for real connection. This practice can be applied to any pair of people!

Everyone deserves deep connection that creates a safe space for vulnerability which leads to profound intimacy.

And sex, of course! Really great sex!

We have the capacity to experience connected, intimate, freeing, soul-nourishing erotic fulfillment.

We long to relax into pleasure in the arms of a caring lover, and we have the ability to create it.

No, it is not just a fantasy!

For those that want this, THE GREAT CIRCLE OF DESIRE delivers.

AND.

Be aware that *this book might not be for you!*

Even though you are reading this now, you may not be able to share these practices with someone else if you have personal healing to do.

As you read through this book, notice your feelings and take care of yourself. It's absolutely true that this practice can heal the deepest wounding of the heart. However, some may need other healing or therapy before opening to this intimate level. Trust your instincts. Really. Take care of yourself.

The great part is, you can do this alone as a healing practice to both sensitize your body to subtle energies and find the love you have for *yourself.* Then you can share it.

When we are in love with ourselves, we attract the beautiful lovers we long for.

Oh, and by the way... I think this is pretty important to share.

Nearly a century ago, one of the top ten best-selling self-help books of all time was written about building wealth. It is a staple for business people everywhere, a favorite in college and university business courses, and is also the primary inspiration behind the popular "Law of Attraction" with Jerry and Esther Hicks.

Many sex educators have embraced the most powerful attribute of this work and made it a central theme of their teachings. This is for a very good reason.

It took two decades of research to discover the top 13 principles of the wealthiest men in the world. Of these principles, the very most important, far above number two on the list, was quite a surprise. The studies proved that the most powerful attribute for developing wealth is a partnership in which couples are able to keep their erotic love alive and strong for a lifetime. It was found that romantic love and sex together elevate men to their highest genius and inspire their greatest contribution to family and society.

In our present day, this "honeymoon style" romance would naturally benefit women in the same way, bringing out their very best. Deep intimacy and connected sex are the super-pleasures that magnify our super-powers for an extraordinary life!

A century ago, women were left with the responsibililty to learn how to keep romance and sex alive for a lifetime - somehow, some way. However, they were not given one clue how to make this happen!

I believe you will find the simple answer in this book. It will surprise you. It's easier (and far more fun!) than taking a walk everyday. It just requires a desire to reap all the amazing benefits!

I welcome you to the best years of your life…

PART ONE - You Want It. You CAN Have It.
PART TWO - What it is and How to DO IT
PART THREE - Practices and Challenges

1

What is DESIRE?

You've been thinking about it for several days now, between the things you do, it sneaks into your mind, teasing, and taunting you.

You want it. You want it bad.

You try to put it off, for whatever reason, doing something else first, but it's persistent.

Your thoughts drift back to the last time you had it, the complete satisfaction and pleasure, all senses satisfied. You feel your body respond to the memory. It was so good.

Desire.

You find yourself wanting it again, those sensations of pleasure are calling you. That's it, you can't take it anymore.

Anticipation. Craving. Desire.

So much desire!

A sigh escapes your lips. You get in your car and drive across town. The miles pass, the desire intensifies, you know how soon you'll have it.

You arrive at your destination, so ready to be fulfilled.

You are greeted with a warm smile and shown to your table.

The server arrives, and warmly smiles at you, "The usual?"

They know.

You nod, and smile back, "Yes, please."

Before long a warm plate arrives.

Tacos.

But not just tacos, a beautiful, lovingly prepared selection of 3 completely uniquely prepared tacos. One is salmon, the next carne asada, and the last shredded chicken.

They arrive on a bright, festive talavera plate, nestled next to spanish rice and black beans.

Between the rice and beans is a pile of bright pico de gallo, garnished with 3 perfectly cut radish roses. It is a work of art to look at, and you know it tastes just as incredible.

Your mouth waters as you pick up the first one.

The warm, corn tortilla is lightly grilled, and filled with chili rubbed, seared salmon. Brightly colored, fresh mango and cilantro salsa adds the perfect balance of sweet and spicy. A light chipotle aioli has been drizzled across the top.

Oh. My.

The combination of aromas and flavors light up your senses. Warm juice drips to the plate. You find yourself expressing sounds of pleasure. Mmmmmm. Ohhhhhhh…

You notice the texture and tart flavor of the diced mango, mingling in the pungent cilantro leaves, like little bright fireworks in contrast to the savory salmon.

Perfection. You're in bliss, true enjoyment, slowly taking each bite into your mouth and savoring it, appreciating it.

It's so good.

You can't help it, and take out your phone and snap a photo of your plate, with your hand holding the first half eaten taco.

With a chuckle, you think... *If only a photo could convey the enjoyment I'm having right now... How could this POSSIBLY be any better?*

I'll have these leftovers later in a warm bath...

Be honest. Do you want tacos now? Do you enjoy your food *this much*? Do you let your desire drive you toward what you want?

Did you ever consider that this level of desire and pleasure was possible from TACOS?!

If not, my friend, you've been missing out.

This is what desire, connection, and appreciation of your food can look like.

Our sensuality, and using our senses fully turns us on, which brings that warm happy feeling of aliveness all day.

Can you see the difference between driving through Taco Bell and grabbing a bunch of stuff and eating it unconsciously, and actually experiencing your food as a sensual experience?

We crave to experience life fully, enjoy all of our senses and share that experience with others.

We want to feel... Aliveness.

It's amazing to hear, "You're so... alive!"

Why are we so attracted to people who are alive and turned on?

They are flowing this energy of aliveness, and they aren't afraid to share it. Think about it...

We share pictures of delicious and beautiful food on social media because we want to convey the pleasure we are having. It feels safe to enjoy food and let others see it.

AND.

If we shared pictures of ourselves enjoying sexual pleasure, we'd be thrown in social media jail! Although the enjoyment is very similar, society has decided what is not okay to make public.

Luckily, we have each other. If you are reading this, you are already connected to people who will celebrate your sensuality, and cheer on your pleasure! Did I mention the Facebook group yet? Check the resources page in back to connect!

Back to this thought... Let yourself feel it.

What food do you crave?

To-die-for designer chocolates melting on your tongue, with outrageous flavor combinations you adore?

Is it the universal favorite... pizza? Sizzling hot, savory sauce and your favorite toppings piled high and nestled into bubbling cheese on a tantalizing crust and baked to perfection?

Or does a softened, drippy pint of gourmet ice cream from two guys in Vermont, with chunks and swirls of sweet lusciousness get your passion flowing? Or just... caramel syrup?

What edible creation makes your mouth water like the mere mention of donuts to Homer Simpson?

Notice how building anticipation for pleasure before it happens is a super-powerful aphrodisiac. Building desire causes physical reactions that prepare us to fully appreciate and experience the most delectable and memorable moments of our lives, embedding a sensual association we can keep coming back to.

It makes life more ... delicious!

We can practice approaching our partners like this. What would your night be like if you spent the day appreciating all of the things that you adore about your partner? How would you see them differently in the evening if you had been feeling grateful all day and thinking about their touch, the sound of their voice, or the comfort and safety of their embrace?

Our minds can create the best or worst in any experience, so why not look for all the good stuff?

Enjoy a donut like Homer would.

Stop what you are doing at sunset, and notice the light and colors change and play over the clouds. Be completely present and enjoy what your body is feeling.

Pleasure can be part of every aspect of our lives. Slow down enough to actually allow desire to arise. Open to the possibility of satisfying all of the senses.

What are you seeing, touching, smelling, hearing and tasting right now?

Let me say that again. Simply.

- ❖ Slow down
- ❖ Allow desire and pleasure to arise (and intensify!)
- ❖ Identify the exact things that fulfill you
- ❖ Indulge in satisfying all of the senses
- ❖ Anticipate and focus on enjoyment
- ❖ Imagine ways to enrich each event

This is what I've learned to apply in many aspects of my life and the reason this book is being written! It's SO SIMPLE, yet we tend to rush past, overcomplicate the process and MISS IT COMPLETELY! I'm sure you've heard this before, "Stop and smell the roses."

Have you thought about the deeper meaning?

Ecstasy occurs when we tune in to the sensual and emotional richness of being totally alive.

- ❖ Instead of unconsciously shoving your meal into your face, learn to experience it. Savor it, one bite at a time, inhale deeply, chew slowly. Combine flavors. Notice textures. Make noises. Have a mouthgasm. YUM!
- ❖ Instead of rushing to the next destination, leave early and enjoy the journey. Take side roads. Allow time to stop and take a photo, or maybe sit in the cafe's garden and have a latte. Breathe. Be overwhelmed by beauty.
- ❖ Instead of working so hard to get to the orgasm, be present throughout the whole sexual encounter. You will be the lover that your partner wants to experience again and again.

Slowing down creates an awareness of the present moment that you may have been missing. We are designed to fully enjoy the pleasures of being human.

After all this talk of tuning in and feeling, let's revisit the effect of amplifying and moving energy.

Do you want to sit there and let life pass you by?!

I didn't think so!

To expand sensuality, energy HAS to move. Remember this energy can feel subtle at first and will be easier to sense over time. To physically feel energy moving requires… movement. It requires circulation, activity, and blood flow.

There are a few ways to elevate energy so it's easier to feel. Sound is definitely a great key to start with.

Do you recall being taught to be quiet while young? Seen and not heard? Many adults still carry that training in their life, accepting it as normal. I have news!

- ❖ No one is born repressing their sounds of pleasure or joy
- ❖ It is not, "Just the way you are"
- ❖ Keeping quiet is a learned behavior
- ❖ Silence is based on guilt and shame
- ❖ This behavior represses *all self expression*

Think about a still pond, the surface is like glass. Now imagine dropping a rock into it, and watch the ripples and splashes spread all the way across the surface.

This is what sound does to energy, so if you aren't able to feel anything yet, try making sounds. If letting sound out seems uncomfortable, I suggest trying it in your car, or when you are alone.

Open your mouth and let the sounds of enjoyment escape.

Explore the range of sounds you can make. Get comfortable hearing yourself make sound.

Ohhhh, Aaaaahhhh, mmmmm, yaaaaaaassssssss!

Grrrrrrrrrr... yuuummmmm!

Have you ever been on a roller coaster? Did you tense up, clench the bars and hold your breath, or did you have a blast screaming your head off and throwing your hands in the air? Making noise in sex is so enlivening! The difference in pleasure is like night and day when the sound moves the energy.

I was never the same after I realized the power of making noise during sex. I learned it in just one night, letting my erotic voice open up and run wild and free for four hours of delirious pleasure. Now I hum, tone, talk erotically, yell "I love you!" and purr or even roar when I feel like it. I have wild freedom now, and men LOVE IT!

Your sounds are a HUGE key to success! Without using words, they encourage your partner to continue, and give them feedback on how you are responding. The "yes" starts out as "mmmm hmmm", then advances to "uh huh!" keeps rising to "Yes, yes, yes! Yes, please!" And then becomes, "Oh, my God!" Or even, "Oh, f***!"

Once I figured this out, the soft groan or hum is something I encouraged with all my lovers. It is simply fabulous for turning a ho-hum lovemaking session into an extraordinary one.

Of course, there are times for deep silence, but people need to learn to let it rip, first.

"Make any kind of noise," I would tell my lovers. Some were hesitant, but even the shy ones could usually manage a little groan or hum. As they did, I would touch them in an erotic spot, and the volume naturally increased.

What helped me master the art of pleasuring men, was not imagining what they might be feeling, but asking them to make sound so I would KNOW their level of pleasure. Before I figured that out, a man might have been quiet during the experience, then said, "Well, I didn't really like that."

After asking them to share sound, not only did I have an indication of their level of arousal, but I could play with their energy, bringing it up, then letting it settle and integrate before stimulating it again.

I also asked if they liked it when I made noise. All agreed it was a wonderful thing.

Extra bonus! Not only does the "love hum" indicate pleasure levels, but it is a vibration that affects the mind and body by keeping you in the moment, and focused on sensations. It helps to eliminate outside distractions and super-powers the pleasure.

Being comfortable expressing vocally is an act of generosity that ensures that your lover will be successful with you. Avoid uncertainty and give them that gift.

The confidence that being fully self-expressed creates is beyond what you would ever expect. You remember about confidence, right? It is the number one most attractive quality to both sexes.

Sound = vibration = energy. You want more pleasure? Move the energy.

Here's more ways to amp it up.

- ❖ Learn to breathe. Most people don't breathe deeply, really ever. Spend some time and breathe. It can make a huge difference in your overall well being. Try this simple breath exercise to rebalance your nervous system.

> "Box-breathing". Inhale for a count of 4, hold your breath for the count of 4, exhale for a count of 4, hold your breath for the count of 4. Repeat at least 4 times. This simple practice brings oxygen to your bloodstream and awareness to your present moment. You can use it when things are stressful and nobody will even know you are doing it.

❖ Jump around! Spend a couple minutes moving your body physically, any way that feels good to get your circulation going.

❖ Touch yourself. No, not just masturbating, this means to touch your body as if YOU LOVE IT! Touch your arms like you want a lover to touch you. Give yourself a hug. The simple act of feeling your own skin brings you into your body. Scratch your skin lightly and then more intensely, and notice what you like most. Close your eyes and touch your own face, feel the warmth of your fingertips on your cheeks, and across your forehead. Press your palm on your own cheek. Feels weird? Keep doing it! Pull your hair a little, or massage your feet, anything to increase sensations that feel good.

❖ Be completely present. Try experiencing your next meal instead of just eating it.

> Go back to the beginning of this chapter, and read it, then try it! You might want to order takeout so you can try it at home. Eat without utensils. Lick your fingers, no... *suck your fingers*! Feed yourself as if you are royalty!

❖ Get still. Sit and watch and feel.

> Sit anywhere. Observe everything going on around you. Notice colors, scents, temperatures. Listen, and pick out sounds you hear. Feel your body connecting with the surface you are on. Watch people interact and pay attention to your thoughts and feelings.

It seems so simple, doesn't it? *Let's keep it simple.*

Our natural human design can take us into the deepest intimacy imaginable, unlocking the doorways in our hearts, and connecting us profoundly with each other.

As we leave the stressful thoughts of speed and productivity, competition and achievement behind, we can shift gears and open to that awareness. Life begins to sparkle with the magic we felt as children.

Does it sound crazy? Amazing? Inviting?

It's waiting for you to ask for it.

Maybe you've heard this all before and it is nothing new. Perhaps it hasn't been fully incorporated into your life. That's because it is a change from everything we have been conditioned to believe. We literally have a choice to shift our focus.

You can re-engage with "the missing link" of humanity's next phase of evolution. Through this power your deepest longings are available and attainable if you are willing to be curious and courageous and go for it.

You can have it. All you have to do is be ready with open arms when it arrives!

"We could have an orgasm from the wind on our face if we were that open."

- Seth

It's time to get on with the book…

I'll tell you what, in each chapter, I'll give you a "cliff notes" version first. The point of the chapter, right at the beginning. If you "get it", you can skip to the next chapter. If you don't, you can read the deeper explanations and stories.

My desire is for you to feel more deeply, experience more authentically, and enjoy all aspects of your life with appreciation.

This book is for human beings who are tired of the surface interactions, and want something deeper.

When you learn these practices, you will attract those who also want this deeper connection. Your lovers will feel it. Your world will shift. It is as endless as you are bold.

You want that? Then I WELCOME YOU to The Great Circle of Desire!

2

Getting What YOU Desire

The point: Your unique desires are valid and should be honored and respected. Communication about acting on these desires is the responsibility of both partners. Sexual exploration is natural. Enjoy with integrity! Explore vulnerability, and the presence that feeds your unique desire.

We have the ability to experience and express feelings and emotions like few other species can. One thing most people can agree on is that we desire to feel and share nurturing touch. It has been scientifically proven that without it, we may survive, but often fail to thrive.

Touch, affection and connection
are part of a happy, healthy life.

Some people like physical affection more than others, and practicing The Great Circle of Desire will help you understand how you feel about it. On that note, entering this space of connection with your current lover can take you to new profound levels of intimacy if you haven't been able to get there before. It can solidify your bond and bring you to where you can truly see each other, openly with true compassion.

So, tell me, what do you desire?

Connection? Appreciation? To be desired? A better sex life?

Desire isn't just about sex, remember the tacos? Pleasure isn't just for sex either, it is for all aspects of life. Learning how to practice The Great Circle of Desire won't change you into anybody but your most authentic self. It can show you what you truly desire, and help you find your voice to ask for it.

This is the space where you get to figure out what turns you on. What do YOU like that lights you up?

Are you hiding from what you really want? Ashamed of your preferences or curiosities? Feeling like you might never find a partner?

Discovering your personal turn-ons and interests is an exciting and fun part of the erotic space created from deep intimacy and trust.

Some people have never received permission to explore and experiment with their sexual curiosities and attractions. If that's the case, I'm giving it to you right now.

All you need to do is receive this gift and give it to yourself. You deserve to be flowing with sexual energy which expresses who you are. What lights your fire?

Let's just acknowledge that we all deserve to feel great. The feelings we share when we stoke the fires of sexual passion are a powerful creative fuel that we can use for sex and SO MUCH MORE!

The same energy can:

- ❖ increase your creativity
- ❖ connect you more to your intuition
- ❖ awaken and circulate stagnant energy in the body
- ❖ bring more restful sleep
- ❖ support you in finding your authentic voice
- ❖ improve health and vitality
- ❖ increase genius and productivity
- ❖ and bring feelings of deep peace and contentment!

Being in the space of intimacy that The Great Circle of Desire creates can elevate and increase the life force sexual energy so it moves in waves of bliss between partners for as long as you can stand it. This is an incredibly healing practice...

You can even use this practice when you or your partner are not "in the mood", but would like to have sex. It's like lighting a match and watching it burn, slowly.

Once the desire is flowing between both people, it's easy to initiate sex. Orgasms take you to incredible heights when you learn to surrender to the flow of bliss together! So, how do we get to this flow of bliss?

We give and receive. We get vulnerable. We let our desires flow. We accept whatever comes up as a natural part of connection. We speak our desires and feelings of appreciation in the moment if it feels right. We respect and honor each other fully in the moment.

We learn to be completely present with each other. What does it feel like to hear these words from a lover?

"I adore you."
"I love you."
"I feel you."
"I see you."
"You turn me on."
"I've got you."
"I'm here for you."
"I want you."
"I'm yours."
"Thank you."

It's intimate, right?
Using these phrases creates closeness, trust, and appreciation whether you give or receive them.

These two roles of giving and receiving are important because one person is actually *holding* the other, providing safety and support. The other is *allowing* the holding, and letting go, surrendering, and trusting their partner.

When we get to the actual practice, it will be explained as a man holding a woman, but I recommend you try both roles, just to explore both sides of giver and receiver. Learn the basics, then make it your own.

In many cases, the deepest places of our hearts have rarely been touched, leaving a sadness and longing for something we aren't quite sure exists. With this simple practice, these places will be awakened. Switches flipped on, energy flowing, ecstasy exploding!

What would it be like to end the disconnect and come back together in a powerful way?

We want it so much, whether single or partnered, and thanks to the advances in technology, we have access to thousands of people, yet seem to have lost our ability to relate to each other in person.

The digital environment of social media and dating apps makes interaction seem "safer" but true intimacy is usually not achieved.

Have you experienced a miscommunication during texting, where you didn't have a true connection, so your mind filled in all the blanks with false information? EEK!

It can escalate into chaos fast!

Think about a time when you were talking on the phone, hearing the voice of your lover, and the emotion, tone and inflections that voice conveyed. That's vulnerability. Honesty.

We can communicate in person, or over distance, but for a real connection the lines have to be open.

Dating apps can make finding someone to connect with so frustrating.

Swiping right based on a visual response from a photo creates an illusion of chemistry. And the photos are often carefully chosen to portray who they want you to see, not who they are.

We disqualify people based on things that may not actually be deal breakers when we are attached to someone looking a certain way or having certain traits. This is also assuming people are portraying themselves honestly...

When you actually meet, how many times is that person someone much different from who they advertised? Was the idea of them in your mind creating a desire that wasn't fully accurate when you met in person? Did the desire for sex outweigh the reality that this person is already lying to you? Did you go for the disconnected sexual gratification anyway?

Maybe. Because it's better than nothing, right?

Maybe. But what if you could feel completely satisfied, even if it's a one time encounter?

We can still go deep and get very intimate together! We can enter what I call, "The Erotic Now". This is a place where time and space disappear and all you feel is peaceful bliss and pure love and connection. It creates a space of intimacy and vulnerability, and can lead to beautiful, connected sex. It acknowledges both people are aligned in the moment, and honor each other.

I know that whether we spend a night with someone or a few months, or a lifetime, we use The Great Circle of Desire, and other connection practices

in this book to connect the heart space and share deep intimacy to get to The Erotic Now.

When dating, when we have these tools, we can speak up, be honest and real, and see if a "date" can meet us powerfully enough to share that space. It opens the possibility of having powerful, intimate encounters no matter how long they last.

The desire for connected sex has grown, and thankfully there is an answer.

So... Do you want better connections?

Are you ready to be part of a new way of loving?

Are you willing to try it?

From what I can see, there are two main types of sex, "disconnected" and "connected"

Let's have a look!

3

The Two Types of Sex

The point: People have sex in many ways, but the underlying theme is that it's one of two types. The first type is connected, warm, nurturing and open (some might call it "making love").
The second type is disconnected, mechanical and cold. Yes, it can bring temporary physical relief, but is missing something. What type do you prefer and practice?

Learning the difference between the two types of sex has changed my entire understanding of quality relationships, whether they last one night or longer. Keep in mind, you can have a connected "quickie" or a disconnected, yet long sex session.

Which of these sounds more like your sex life, or the one you'd like to have?

Disconnected Sex:

- ❖ No conversation or agreements
- ❖ Basic steps: Kiss, fondle, penetrate, climax
- ❖ Like masturbating by using someone else's body
- ❖ Priorities are pleasurable sensations and a physical release
- ❖ Functional, and mechanical like a biological need
- ❖ Ten to twenty minutes from start to finish
- ❖ After climax, leaves both feeling more isolated
- ❖ Often begins with surface attraction, rarely goes deeper
- ❖ One partner always in the lead

Connected Sex:

- ❖ Often begins with emotional connection or friendship
- ❖ Is even more satisfying with communication and agreements
- ❖ No set formula, allowed to flow within boundaries
- ❖ Focuses on the combined pleasure of both partners
- ❖ Goals are mutual enjoyment, and authentic expression
- ❖ Heals stress, loneliness and isolation
- ❖ Can be long leisurely hours of caring and nurturing bliss
- ❖ Complete presence with partner, regardless of duration
- ❖ Full body pleasure leaves both partners feeling fulfilled and opened to joy and love.
- ❖ Partners take turns giving and receiving, allowing full surrender for each
- ❖ Trust and vulnerability, lead to curiosity and creativity
- ❖ Compassionate and healing, honoring each other
- ❖ Comfort to ask questions in the moment, or shift direction

It took a lot of trial and error to fully understand this distinction. Fumbling through bad relationships can teach us a lot if we can learn from the experiences instead of repeating them endlessly.

Trying to figure it out with a partner who isn't present with us is very frustrating.

My search for answers took me back to my first marriage. I was almost twenty years old. After the initial excitement of a new relationship and a wedding, we were... married.

After only three months, he stopped desiring sex with me regularly. After a year, I desperately tried to communicate that I needed more intimacy from my husband, but we had lost any real connection we once had. He was fine with disconnected sex, and even when I tried to tell him how I felt cold and empty, it never changed.

I was talking to deaf ears. After wondering if he was insane or I was insane, I decided he couldn't possibly love me. The truth was that he didn't have the ability or tools to hear me.

When I asked him to take his time with me and kiss me more affectionately and touch me with tenderness, he had no idea what that meant.

I was confused, angry and frustrated that my husband could not hear me or feel me. He was limited by what he learned from TV and pornography and didn't realize that sex required intimacy and connection to keep me feeling loved and appreciated.

I longed for connection, to be heard, seen, and known deeply. I wanted to be appreciated and to feel tenderness. I craved to open and discover ecstasy with him, and it just wasn't happening. The slow and exciting foreplay that took hours before marriage was now gone and had turned into a pattern that was predictable and all too brief.

I couldn't feel comfortable. I had bought into the popular idea that a man was supposed to lead. It was his desire and passion that should always be more powerful than mine. Sex was supposed to be his idea.

As much as I wanted to initiate sex, I didn't dare. I might be looked at as a slut, or worse, taking over could cost him his masculinity and wound his ego, perhaps irreparably.

I didn't feel sexy or desired, and the sex was short. After a few minutes of manual stimulation, he always gave up. Nothing was said, because I was embarrassed that I couldn't orgasm on the spot and didn't know how to tell him what to do to bring me pleasure.

I realize now that I didn't know myself well enough then, but at that time, how could I have done it differently?

That was 40 years ago.

Back then, a tiny trickle from the bathtub faucet was my only reliable source for a little orgasm, and it took a while to get there. I couldn't admit that, let alone ask him to spend at least 20 minutes giving me a focused delicate touch like the water did. He was usually done in a few minutes!

People didn't talk much about women having orgasms. It was all so secretive back then, and seemed like a mystery. I had nobody to talk with or learn from.

I was so frustrated, feeling like he refused to listen to me, that I blamed him, stopped having sex entirely, and slept on the couch.

Does this sound like anyone you know?

My pleas for marriage counseling were ignored. Looking back, I understood that he didn't want to talk about his feelings and be embarrassed or judged for his lack of sexual understanding under the scrutiny of a shrink. At this time, it just seemed like he didn't care.

What to do? We were stuck.

I found myself being a victim, full of anger, sadness and resentment.

We lived as roommates with no intimacy and I waited for him to change. In my loneliness, I began looking for connection elsewhere. It wasn't long before I had a brief petting session with the next-door neighbor who had always shown interest in me. He gave me the attention I craved and made me feel important. This left me full of guilt.

With the lack of connection and complete absence of sexual intimacy, my husband became full of rage, and used alcohol to numb himself. He simply had no idea what to do with me and was powerless.

He threatened violence on several occasions. Full of depression, I became afraid of him. I no longer felt safe in my own home. It wasn't long before we were divorced. I would have to find someone that understood what I needed a little bit better than that.

I thought I knew what I wanted but did not feel the freedom to express it. Maybe the truth was that I wasn't even sure what I truly needed. It was confusing and difficult.

This scenario is not uncommon. Lack of intimacy can often lead to depression, loneliness, addiction and violence. In desperation, reaching out to others to fill the emptiness can leave us with the burden of guilt and shame. With no answers, many end up divorced like I did.

Think about your past relationships and how you navigated through them. Did you learn and grow? Do you repeat old patterns? Did you own your part of the story?

The three following stories are examples that many people can relate to on the journey from disconnected to connected sex. They may bring up uncomfortable feelings if you realize you have not been able to state your truth and ask for what you want. See if you relate to any part of the following examples.

Partner One – Pete, The Stone Wall
After our date, I invited Pete to come home with me. The ruggedly handsome man had been flirting with me suggestively all night.

I was turned on mentally, imagining his hands on me.

As soon as we got inside the front door, we began kissing, and things progressed quickly. His hands skimmed over me, too fast, I didn't feel warmth or like he was even aware of me. I wanted to slow down and be held, so I wrapped my arms around him, hoping he would do the same.

I felt *nothing.*

His heart and chest were like a stone wall. I pressed against him, seeking warmth or comfort, and only felt cold and repelling. He might as well have had a neon sign flashing "CLOSED".

This wasn't my first rodeo, but it threw me off.

He hadn't touched me during our date, just made suggestive comments, and undressed me with his eyes. I thought he was into me, but this wasn't working.

My heart sank, and my nerves were on edge. He led me to the couch, and as he removed my clothes, I wanted to run away, but was too embarrassed to stop him. He kept kissing me with no feeling.

The stone wall of a man continued the disconnected sex formula, much the same as my ex-husband had, decades earlier.

Kiss, fondle, penetrate, climax.

My mind raced about what I really wanted, and worried about him not using a condom, wondering if he was just going to ejaculate in me. I wanted to push him off and scream, but not a sound escaped my lips.

I let him finish his process, feeling like he had just used my body to masturbate with, like I wasn't even there... He had pulled out at the very end, leaving his semen on my belly. I had shut down, and he didn't even notice. He didn't even make eye contact, just got dressed quickly and excused himself, promising to call.

Sure.

I felt dirty, and used.

Gross.

I stood in the shower, crying, trying to rinse the feelings away.

For the next three days I was numb, I called into work, and curled up in the fetal position in my bed. I checked in with my body for an answer. Its response was shocking but clear.

I felt... raped.

Rape is a strong word, so I looked for more clarification. Yes I did feel like a victim, humiliated and degraded, used like a piece of meat and tossed away. But how could I feel raped when I had consented to having sex with him?

I thought about it. I only "consented" because we didn't talk about it. Because I brought him home, it was *assumed* we would have sex.

He didn't ask, I didn't say yes or no.

I allowed it. I allowed him to "rape" me, which wasn't true rape, but nonetheless, felt horrible. It was something I could have prevented if I had felt empowered to speak up. He didn't even know how I was feeling, and of course, never called. It was likely that he did this to women regularly, only thinking of himself.

How many women don't know how to say no,

so saying nothing becomes yes?

How many men assume that her saying nothing means it's okay?

I spent time healing, and resolved to wait to have sex again, until I met a man who felt warm, comforting, and open.

Partner Two - Ben, The Big Chill

I stuck to my word and waited to feel something before having sex again. I went on several dates and made sure to initiate a hug so I could discern how open a man was.

I began to feel the difference between open and closed hugs.

One of the men I was out with was a writer named Ben. He showed up in a pair of jeans and a nice shirt and jacket. Sexy, put together but not overdone. Nice. He was funny and pleasant.

After our first date, I asked for a hug. He pulled me into a warm embrace, took a deep breath in, and let it out in a sigh.

Ohhhh. That was nice.

He stood there with me, and seemed to have no intention of letting go. Now that I was close I inhaled his scent, clean, and subtle like a pine forest. It was wonderful, warm and comforting.

I relaxed fully, and my body responded, desire rising, and heard myself asking him to come home with me.

He declined, said he had to be up early, but maybe next time. Ben held me for a while longer before giving me a light kiss and saying goodnight. He looked into my eyes, and smiled. I melted.

As he drove away, I felt great! My imagination considered the experience and explored what sex with him would be like, so caring, and loving...

The fantasy kept me warmed up until our next date a few nights later. We had a great time and he did come home with me as he said he would.

You can imagine my confusion when things shifted at my house.

His kiss was warm and he held me in a nice embrace. I was falling into bliss when he suddenly began to kiss me differently.

The Big Chill.

He pulled his energy back and became more dominating and cold. I felt as if he was taking from me.

NOT THIS AGAIN!

I allowed him to have sex with me, trying to find the warmth again, but he had pulled his emotions all back inside and was only focusing on the physical sensations. It was like he could do one or the other.

Tears welled up. I was *not* okay with it.

It was time to get brave, so as he finished getting his pleasure and release, I thought about what to say. He didn't notice I had shut down.

After he was done, he rolled to the side. Forcing myself, I opened my mouth, sharing that I felt used.

That woke him up.

His reaction was confusion. Understandable. I had not expressed what I wanted or stopped him, and unhappy with the result, tried to blame him.

He looked at me coldly, and asked, "So what do you want me to do?"

His tone was flat, and I felt unsafe to say anything. He was asking me to be responsible for what I wanted, but I felt shut down.

So many words flooded into my brain, pushing to the front, wanting my mouth to say them.

"Love me and care about me and hold me close, make me feel wanted and be warm and open like you were the other night!"

My lips pressed together tighter and nothing came out. I wanted to cry, and scream, but all I could do was apologize. Then I asked him to leave. I felt hurt again and realized I needed to figure this out.

Why did I attract men who followed the formula for disconnected sex?

Kiss, fondle, penetrate, climax.

This was not the sex I wanted to have, so what was I supposed to be learning?

I contemplated some reasons that this "Big Chill" was happening.

- ❖ Shame or guilt
- ❖ Sex seen as dirty
- ❖ Fear of intimacy
- ❖ Lack of emotional intelligence
- ❖ Old patterns, they don't know any different
- ❖ Missing trust or communication.
- ❖ No desire for relationship at all
- ❖ Plain old selfishness

There had to be men in the world who could connect!

Something just didn't add up. A thought crossed my mind. Could it even be possible that *maybe they didn't even know how women felt?*

Did anyone even *want* to connect, or listen to me? Was I doing something wrong?

I went back to healing myself, therapy, and again, resolved to wait to initiate a new connection until I felt strong love for myself.

Partner 3 - Randy, Three's the Charm

Months went by. A friend suggested that I meet her cousin Randy. I don't usually like matchmakers, but she said he was a good guy.

I didn't expect this "good guy" to turn into another situation with a stone walled chest. I had no idea that I was about to have a defining moment.

It was easy to spot Randy at the park, he wore a navy blue sweater that fit perfectly, and a dark brown scarf.

He smiled warmly and shook my hand, which seemed a bit reserved at first before I remembered that taking it slow was the key.

I tuned into how I felt with him as we walked and talked for a while. He was much taller and bigger than me, but matched my pace, walking right next to me.

He seemed cautious. Or was that me being cautious?

I missed being touched, and looked at his big, strong hands as he gestured while he talked.

I imagined his hands on my body and felt a warmth spread through my heart.

We crossed a small bridge, and the path turned left around the lake into a grove of trees.

He took my hand gently in his as we walked and continued to talk. Nice, and warm, his grip was comforting and solid. I noticed we were out of view of other people, when he pulled me into his arms.

Um, okay.

Though he was a strong tall man, the embrace felt a bit awkward and mechanical. He leaned in to kiss me, and I let him, doing my best to bring the warmth and open heart to our moment.

Then I stopped and pulled back.

I explained to Randy how I didn't feel connected yet, and how I wanted to feel his heart before we kissed. He was definitely shocked.

He didn't understand, and of course, felt blamed. It was horribly awkward. I began to pull away, and he gently stopped me, and asked me to help him understand how I felt.

I asked him to just hold me while I talked. He did.

When I explained the three days of dark depression following the encounter with Pete, he was sincerely concerned.

He had no idea of the pain that a woman can experience from these mechanical encounters, and asked me how he could be better at it.

Wow!

How could they change this behavior if they don't know the pain it causes? Men are not oriented to understand a woman's emotions, any more than a woman knows a man's perspective.

We need to learn about each other.

We need to talk in the moment.

We all know that something has to change so we can be better at this. But what?

Randy sincerely wanted to help. That meant that if I figured out the problem, he would be happy to fix it. This was obviously a nice guy that did not want to hurt me or any woman intentionally. I had to admit that many of the men before him were this way too, but I didn't know how to talk to them.

I decided right then to end the withholding, and be bold.

What came into my mind was to ask him to love me. I paused, took a deep breath, and considered the gravity that people attach to the word "love". When I started speaking, the perfect words came out.

I asked if he would be willing to do a little experiment.

He eagerly nodded. I asked him to hold me close in a firm embrace and just *appreciate me* while I hugged him back and relaxed into him.

He wrapped his arms around me, and pulled me into his chest.

In stillness, I felt his caring heart welcome me in. I melted into him and felt so happy. The gentle tenderness I craved overcame me, and tears fell down my cheeks. He held me firmly but gently while I closed my eyes in surrender.

It felt so good.

I felt the open flow of appreciation between us and my body began to open and desire sex with him.

When I shared with him that his gentle embrace was opening my desire to make love with him, he was surprised again. He said he wanted to wait before we did that, and just enjoy the feeling we were sharing. That feeling was "The Erotic Now"!

He looked into my eyes, and kissed me again. My entire body responded with tingly sparkles as I felt the desire flow between us. The kiss was now warm, and delicious.

We breathed deeply together, allowing the pleasure to increase, and he whispered in my ear, *"I get it, thank you."*

Wow.

"Making women happy is so easy. Why didn't I know about this earlier?"
- Randy, 35, Phoenix

The next time we met, I felt comfortable telling him how I was feeling, and asking for what I really wanted. We did make love, it built slowly, lasted hours, and left us both completely fulfilled.

We talked, and laughed and asked each other questions throughout the time we spent, learning about each other's desires and turn-ons.

Randy and I became lovers for a while, but more so, we became close friends. I felt safe with him, and we explored with each other fearlessly.

We even traded giver and receiver roles! I didn't know how much men needed to be held and appreciated so they could heal just like women. Randy and I had a trust I had not experienced before. What a breakthrough!

I felt the importance of this understanding, of how we can hold each other and heal together.

Wow!

In all of my relationships, the problem had been in the inability to connect. And the solution was SO SIMPLE. The right kind of hug.

The hardest part was asking for it. It took time to become fluid in all situations, but the practice was a joy. After doing The Power Embrace with many men, I could easily feel the intimacy and tenderness that I longed for my whole life.

My body relaxed and opened as sensuality and desire came alive. I fell in love every time, and the pleasure was so overwhelming, I couldn't get enough. I felt safe to express more and ask for my desires to be fulfilled. I was in paradise!

I was able to enter The Erotic Now more easily each time, with any partner!

Time and time again I experienced:

- ❖ Frustration and stress shifting easily to sensuality and contentment.
- ❖ Relaxation allowed slowing down to focus on pleasure, rather than a rush to "climax".
- ❖ Trust, respect, honor, and love are alive and present.
- ❖ Increased intimacy, feeling seen, known and understood.
- ❖ Lovemaking begins with satisfaction and fulfillment
- ❖ Vulnerability and authenticity blossom
- ❖ Expression of pleasure becomes more free
- ❖ Confidence develops
- ❖ Creativity, fun and exploration become natural
- ❖ Passion and desire increase
- ❖ Sexual trauma, wounding, shame and guilt fade and heal
- ❖ A solid foundation of connection and relatedness brings comfort and security

After this shift, I knew I would never

tolerate disconnected sex or relationships again!

I found my voice to ask for the slow connection, and building of desire. After experiencing it the first time, my lovers returned to me with open arms. They knew that welcoming me into a warm embrace almost always ended in incredible sex.

It was all about connecting the energy in our bodies, and opening enough to let it flow.

Polarity is the key to connected sex. The next section will teach the basics of polarity, and then we will get into the actual practice of The Great Circle of Desire.

Take your time with this, and let yourself open to it. Everyone is different, find your pace to explore. Do some journaling or meditation if feelings arise on your journey to new levels of ecstasy!

The last section of this book covers other details like settings, unique situations, and "troubleshooting".

If you need support, have questions, or just want to share your journey, please join the conversation in The Great Circle of Desire Facebook Group. (Resources in the back of the book.)

In love, 100x120cm, oil on canvas, by Ines Honfi

PART ONE - You Want It. You CAN Have It

PART TWO - What it is and How to DO IT

PART THREE - Practices and Challenges

4

Understanding Polarity, Attraction and Flow

"But there is no energy unless there is a tension of opposites..."

- C.G. Jung

The point: To understand how the practice works, you need to first distinguish the ideas of magnetism and polarity. This book is written to a heterosexual audience based primarily on masculine and feminine polarity. This is to keep it simple and easy to understand. It does apply regardless of your gender orientation, or sexual preferences if you can use the giver (masculine) and receiver (feminine) model for your relationship.

Let's talk about this polarity thing and the basics of masculine and feminine energies. While reading, notice if you lean toward masculine or feminine, regardless of your physical body.

The Masculine Polarity/Power + positive/giving/outward/constant

Imagine men as the sun. The sun has one job, to shine, non-stop. The masculine power is single-focused. How do men relate to the sun?

- ❖ Desiring and penetrating the earth (feminine)
- ❖ Giving life to all, providing love in the form of light and heat

❖ Supplying energy in many forms to enhance the feminine power's creations

Imagine in this analogy that human men receive energy from the sun, or above. The energy flows down the center of the body to arrive at the genitals where it builds plasma energy inside of them. It is literally, life force energy. A powerful, primal desire for the female creates an urge to release this energy into her genitals.

The perfect design of the man is that he is very focused on sex and longs to share this energy. It is normal for a man to be proud of his penis and he wants to know he gives a woman pleasure. The whole idea of sending penis photos originates from the power he feels in this organ. His quest is to find a woman who wants the love, support and sexuality he has to give.

When women can understand, appreciate and receive this desire, men can operate in their true design.

"Once I saw the basic design of men and women, I had a kind of instant awakening. I could never emasculate men again, having found a new compassion for them!"

- Angela, 37, Tucson

A man's desire to express his gift of sexual desire is perfectly normal and healthy.

He deserves to be honored for this natural design and the desire that comes with it, every bit as much as the woman wants to be honored for the beauty and love radiating from her heart.

When he finds a woman who is open to him, he provides massive amounts of energy for her creations. Most obviously, this is for producing children and providing and protecting for them. Sometimes this looks like financial, emotional, or other forms of support. The masculine power is the provider and protector, the hero archetype, who is willing to risk his life for those he cares about or a worthy cause. Think about the weight of that!

As women, the best gift we can give is to be receptive and give him space to be that powerful sacred masculine.

No matter how powerful a woman is, there is great strength in allowing a man to take care of her.

The Feminine Polarity/Power - negative/receiving/inward/flowing
Imagine women as the earth. The earth has many facets to her job. She is a complex system who supports and nurtures millions of life forms. Women are multi-focused and complex. How do women relate to the earth?

❖ Receiving the sun's life-giving rays
❖ Nurturing and sustaining our human bodies
❖ Creating and balancing many biological systems

The energy from the earth flows up the female torso to arrive at the heart where she builds energy to give back to the man. Women experience this as nurturing energy, and have a strong desire to take care of things. She longs to give appreciation to the masculine power to thank him for all he gave to her. The feminine power is nurturing and loving.

These two powers work together in a cycle.

The Great Circle of Desire moves in this circular fashion. The male seeks to move his energy into the female genitals and the female seeks to move her energy into the male heart.

So what does this mean?

The Power Embrace will complete the electrical design already in place to flow through the heart and genitals, creating a full circle, as pictured. When the energy is flowing, both partners can open into a vulnerable connection.

The design inherent in the animal kingdom has a simple, natural polarity between males and females to ensure the species evolves and survives. In most cases, females look for a male to provide for and protect them so they can raise their young safely.

Male birds have brighter feathers and put on quite a show to attract a female. When he wins the right to mate with her, he will fiercely protect her from other males and predators. Her design is less colorful to ensure she can stay camouflaged and protect her young. Nature's design is perfect.

Most of the creatures on this Earth follow their attraction and polarity without worrying what anyone will think. But how do humans do it?

Welllllll, we often overthink it.

We are all unique in our attractions and sexual desires, but sometimes believe we must conform to the old societal standards and expectations. Isn't it interesting that when we are able to be honest about who we are attracted to, and how we feel, we can more readily connect with each other?

When we learn to distinguish our own heart's wisdom, we are present with who we are and what we truly desire. Then, we can find lovers and mates who do the same.

AND.

We are complex emotional beings, so sometimes this gets messy. With so many choices, so many options, and a world full of adventure and opportunity, we question ourselves endlessly, wondering if our choices were the right ones. Do we want a standard relationship or something entirely new and unique?

Our animal friends seem to accept their nature without question and live in unconditional love. They appear to make choices and live spontaneously without concern or regret.

This same flow is available to humans when we allow masculine and feminine energy to entwine.

Have you seen the 6-sided star before? Most are aware of it, but don't realize it is the symbol of balanced male and female energies, and the symbol of the #4 heart chakra. The female triangle receives energy from the earth at the lowest singular point and expands its reach upward and outward through the breasts and into the sun/sky. The male triangle receives energy from the highest singular point above, expanding down and outward through the genitals to penetrate the earth. This is another example of the masculine and feminine, sun/sky and earth making love with each other in balance and harmony. As people are learning to tap into the natural flow of their heart energy, they are discovering a new happiness.

As the heart center in the middle of the chest is activated through this practice, a beautiful feeling arises.

It can feel like tingling, warmth, or love, and as some have expressed to me, even fireworks!

Like a jumpstart, our hearts return to life, and however you label it, it feels good!

"I don't ever want this feeling to end!" - Hary, 27

Adoration, 100x120 cm, oil on canvas, by Ines Honfi

Electricity Means Pleasure

I was just watching a video by Dr. Bruce Lipton. He declared that the body is a battery, and each cell holds 1 ½ watts of electrical power.
Scientists estimate the number of cells to be somewhere around 50 trillion. Therefore we have approximately 75 trillion watts stored inside of our bodies. Holy cow that's a lot!

Almost all of us have seen a martial artist throwing a man against the wall without touching him. We have all heard of the faith healers that send some kind of "divine" energy into a follower's forehead who claims it changed their lives.

Reiki healing energy from the hands is becoming well-known, and even showing up in hospitals as a supportive addition to western medicine. Some specially trained people have even learned to start fires with the energy from their hands.

In the movie Bruce Almighty, we saw Bruce give his girlfriend an orgasm from the next room without touching her!

So realistically, how do we apply this energy to pleasure?

Some may have discovered what they would call "profound love" while using alcohol, popular drugs or plant medicines. This feeling is easier to access because the altered state overrides our "inhibitions" right? Our bodies open up and the electricity flows unobstructed between us. Our fears magically disappear, so we can skip past establishing trust, connection and vulnerability and feel enough freeedom and desire to have sex with wild abandon. It feels fantastic!

Then in the morning... what happens?

How can we feel so open and full of confidence one night, just to return to our same-old ways until the next time we alter our consciousness? How do we access that while present and sober?

The Great Circle of Desire allows the natural electricity between bodies to be accessed through intention without stimulants. I mean, by creating a specific electrical circuit with another, we generate pleasure we didn't know was possible. The very real experience of deep connection is within reach.

When energy moves between bodies, it creates a wonderful feeling of soothing love and warmth.

Some people have entered the experience through slow dancing or cuddling, or simply focusing on how much they love their partner. We will use an exact method that creates results consistently.

So, how does it work? We have positive and negative charges in our body. When we align them, without fear and unobstructed, the energy moves. It's really that simple.

And it's time for more people to understand how to do it! You in?

The Power Embrace's Polarity and Magnetics

People have 7 natural energy centers in their physical body. These are sometimes called chakras, energy centers, or vortexes. The alignment of just 2 of these centers can allow the other 5 to open, connect and flow, allowing for new and amazing sensations.

It's sort of magical, but actually more like science. You don't need to study this, just trust it's there.

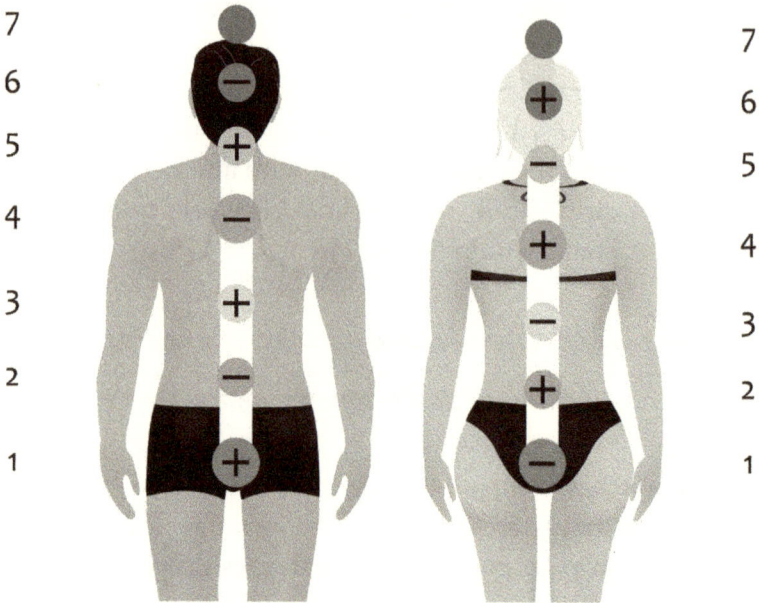

Think about batteries. You know how you have to put them the right way into electronic devices following the little + or -? This is so the energy will run the right way to create power to run the device.

That's polarity. Once you have the batteries in right, do you think about them, or just "turn on" the device, knowing it will work?

Our bodies have the same kind of polarities, and the switch to turn us on is as simple as connecting them to the opposite polarities, just like batteries!

You can observe that men have an outward body part, the penis, which expresses energy outward (including ejaculation) from their positive energy center, #1. It is obvious then, that women pull energy into their genitals at #1.

Women have an outward body part, the breasts, and flow physical energy (as loving, nourishing milk) outward from their positive energy center, #4.

What we are learning more about now is how men pull energy into their body at their heart and how important it is.

We are electrical beings, right? Think about it this way. When the energy between the hearts and genitals of both the male and female are connected, it creates a closed loop circuit. Like being plugged in.

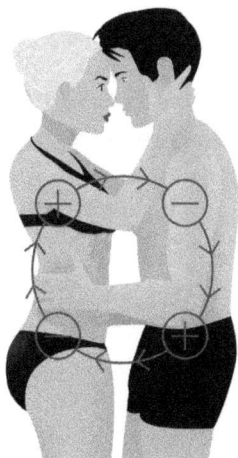

In this connection, you could say they are "running on all 4 cylinders". You want free energy? Here it is! "The Missing Link" is not an ape-man, it is understanding the heart connection.

Some men have explained to me the feeling they get after we "plug in" this way.

"It's like an overwhelming light energy in my chest - it feels like fireworks exploding!"

I told the men that The Power Embrace was everything I needed in order to want to make love with them. The key to having more sex and better sex is through the heart. It is the most under-rated, yet most important sexual organ. This is due to the women's heart center taking a back seat for thousands of years. We put it on the back burner and forgot about it while men did their thing.

Connecting the heart is how the women finally win, and when the women win, the men win, too. Women get the intimacy they need to trust men, and then the sex is mutual exploration of pleasure. We are all in this together.

The most common response from both men and women was

"Why hadn't I realized this before?

How could it be this easy?"

The heart is powerful! We know through extensive scientific research, that it is the largest energy field of the body. We are exploring the possibilities of it with this "heart-fire" orgasm.

We are becoming bedroom scientists! The pleasure is so satisfying, that after the energy settles down, and the penis is remembered, there may not even be a desire for ejaculation.

It blows the minds of many men that sex is about more than genitals. Who among the male readers is interested in a heartgasm?

Ok... just a little more on magnetics and polarity:

Think of the bar magnets you played with in science class as a kid. The same magnetic charges (++ or --) repel each other. It's nearly impossible to get them to touch, let alone stick together.

The opposite charges attract, negative to positive. Those magnetics are in our bodies. When we feel "attracted" to someone, we likely have opposite polarity from them.

Our energies literally WANT to play together if the polarities are right. It's a good place to start.

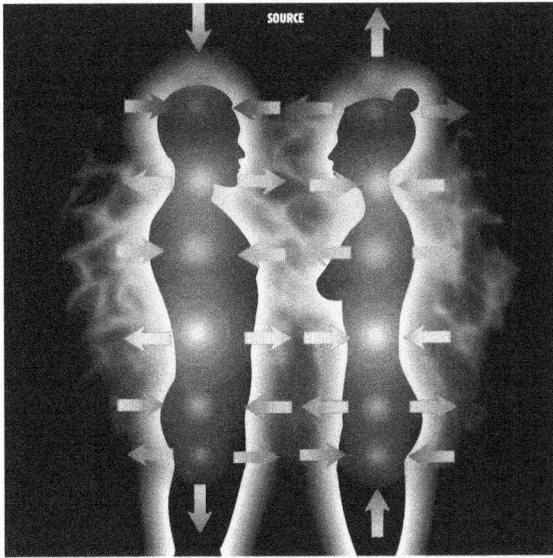

The body radiates energy **out** from the front and back at the positive (+) energy centers.

It pulls energy **in** both sides at the negative (-) energy centers.

When you align these energies, the movement created by these opposing forces creates a flow of energy, and you can amplify it to an orgasmic state of bliss!

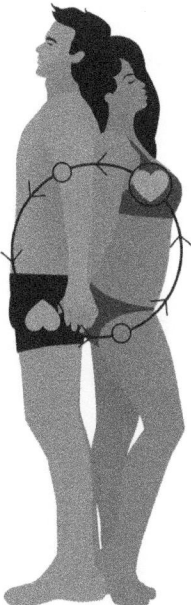

Because the energy flows from both sides, this even works back to back!

For The Power Embrace practice, we will focus on the polarity and movement of energy at the genital center (#1) and the heart center (#4).

Ok, hope I didn't lose you on that. When you understand this, it makes it easier to visualize and feel the flow of energy between you and your partner. If you don't understand it yet, don't worry! You will when you feel it!

You want to know how? I hope so! That's next.

5

The Power Embrace

The point: This is the part where you learn the actual practice, how to "plug in" and get connected. It explains how to physically align with your partner and find the place where you can feel the energy moving. It's like a hug, with much more meaning and feeling.

"We need four hugs a day for survival. We need 8 hugs a day for maintenance. We need 12 hugs a day for growth."

- Family therapist, Virginia Satir

In a world of side hugs, "A frame" hugs, back slapping bro hugs, we need to raise the bar on good hugs!

- ❖ What is your hug experience like?
- ❖ Have you had a hug that lasted 20 seconds?
- ❖ How about longer?
- ❖ Have you let anyone in enough to actually listen to their subtle energies and feel them?
- ❖ Do you resist longer hugs?

The simplest thing has been overlooked by SO MANY PEOPLE!

There is science behind the 20 second hug, and the impact it has on us. Before we get into The Power Embrace, which is essentially a powerful, vulnerable, next-level hug, let's have a look!

Here are some things a nice long hug can do for you:
- ❖ Increase the release of oxytocin (the love hormone)
- ❖ Reduce the production of cortisol (the stress hormone)
- ❖ Lower blood pressure and tension
- ❖ Raise happiness and joy
- ❖ Connect people in deeper ways

Do you want any of that? I KNOW I DO!

So, that's why we are here, in this book together. Because we have a very real human desire to connect, deeply.

The Power Embrace may look like a hug, but it's more like a hug with purpose. A hug that can heal the world!

In a typical hug, hands just kind of go... wherever. With The Power Embrace, we will intentionally place hands where they will amplify the energy flow.
Which hand is your "dominant hand? The dominant hand has a positive (giving) charge, and the less dominant hand has a negative (receiving) charge.

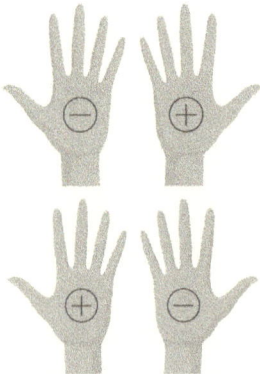

"Right handed" people flow energy out of their right hand.

"Left handed" people flow more energy out of their left hand.

These can be changed through intent but just stick with what is natural for now. If both hands seem equal, try both ways and see if you can feel a difference.

Oh, and you may not be able to feel it at first. It's a subtle thing until you tune into it. Think about a radio dial when you can tell there's music playing but it's fuzzy. When you are new to feeling energy that's what it's like. Once you learn to fine tune, the song becomes clear, and you can feel another person's energy clearly.

Let's do The Power Embrace!

Once you have decided who will be the masculine/giver and feminine/receiver, you can begin The Power Embrace.

When The Power Embrace is working, the first and fourth energy centers (chakras) align and flow. #1 is at the base of the spine, #4 is at the heart. When we focus on these, the rest will naturally connect.

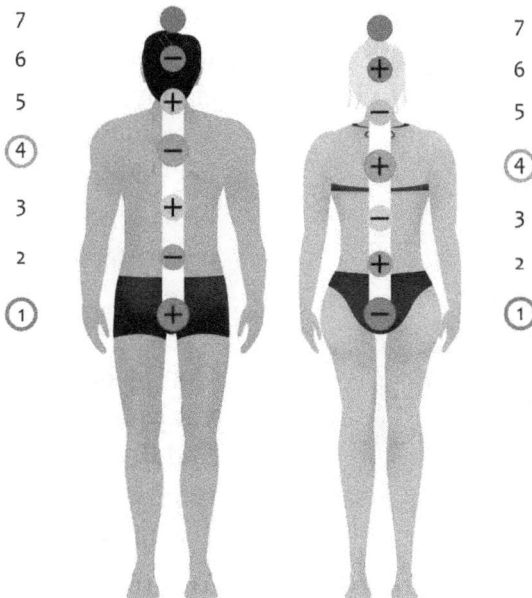

Note about body differences:

What is most important is being able to relax into this embrace so you don't end up with muscle cramps, or limbs falling asleep. It can be pretty awkward at first, but most people can find a comfy space with some adjusting. Sometimes height, weight, and size differences make it challenging. Do your best. If you can't figure it out, check out the alternative positions and options in the last section of the book.

Keep in mind that regardless of physical body, often couples identify differently, or sometimes switch roles. Experiment playing both parts (giver/receiver) and notice what produces the best feelings. That is where energy is flowing the strongest. This can be quite subtle, so take your time. See if you can identify what situations might call for you to be in the opposite role.

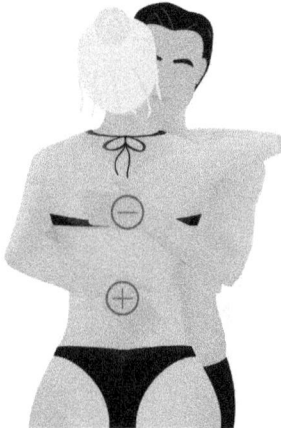

Stand close together, facing each other and the masculine opens his arms, welcoming her in. The feminine moves in closely, wrapping her arms around him. She then places her dominant hand onto his heart center, or as high up as is comfortable on the center of his spine.

Don't worry if you can't reach, you want to be able to relax, so find the most comfortable spot. I like to have my arms under his for the best reach. The palm of the non-dominant hand goes beneath that on his spine, between his heart and waist.

He follows, wrapping his arms around her, with confidence, strength and support. Start with the less dominant hand. Place it on the high center of her back, at her heart center, as you begin The Power Embrace. The exact spot is about 2″ (5 cm) above the clasp of the bra. The plug is about the same size as the center of the palm (conveniently!)

He should move his hand slightly up or down feeling for a shift in energy. Give each spot at least 5-10 seconds or more to sense with your complete focus without moving. Relax and breathe. It is very important for the maximum energy flow. Now place the palm of the dominant hand between the waist and the heart, squarely on the spine.

REMEMBER: If you can't feel the energy, just pick a spot and be still. It is subtle and can take time to tune into.

Be completely present in the moment. This means to shift from focus on worrying and analyzing in the mind to feeling in the body. Begin to think of your partner with gentle caring intent. Think about what you are grateful for. You can also just focus on appreciation for all women or men. Appreciation and connection are the keys, right?

"I felt a whole new possibility for peace between men and women that I'd never seen before. My whole view changed so quickly. I can't wait to use this in all my relationships! "

- Hannah, 25

Through intention, everything that you focus upon and feel will be communicating with all your partner feels, in a dance of sensuality. This communication is the sensual language partners share.

No words need to be spoken. Create a loving intention to release all stress and tension and allow positive, loving and caring feelings to emerge through the process.

Notice how your body feels and adjust so you are comfortable. Once you get into the embrace, you can feel the energy begin to move.

It can be subtle at first. Most people aren't tuned into this subtle level of feeling so be patient and breathe deeply to increase the energy.

If you still can't feel anything, just focus on not overthinking and relax any tension you have in your body. Sometimes trying "too hard" will make it harder to feel.

With each breath, relax a little more and just feel...

"Love is our true destiny. We do not find the meaning of life by ourselves alone - we find it with another."

- Thomas Merton

6

Let The Great Circle of Desire Flow!

*"All the need for guides, books, and "how-to's" fall away
as you touch a place together that is so comfortable, it feels
like home. Intuitively knowing how to fulfill your partner's
needs and desires is simply a natural and flowing awareness."*

- Cosmic Kari

The point: Time to feel! If you've really been doing the cliff notes version of this book and think you are getting it, this will tell you if you've gotten it or not. If you can't feel it, go back and read more.

Like any new practice, getting it dialed in might take a little time. The following suggestions are separated into "for him" and "for her" columns that detail what each partner can explore.

Read through everything first, so you can be less in your mind when you are in the embrace. Allow your innate awareness and intuition to show you what to focus on. Pay attention to your partner's signals and adjust to flow with them.

AND.

Don't overthink it. The flow of The Great Circle of Desire is waiting for you to get out of the way so it can happen as it is designed to.

Once you are in The Power Embrace and The Great Circle of

Desire's energy is flowing, experiment with these:

For Masculine (Giver)	For Feminine (Receiver)
1. Focus on the female (receiver) - Use any form of appreciating that allows you to access a feeling of caring. It can be general, such as "Thank you for trusting me", or "I love holding your beautiful body.", or "Holding you feels so amazing!" For more power, focus on the beautiful being you are with and make it more specific. Be sure that your focus has moved down from thoughts in your mind to feelings in your heart, feeling love, and allowing your heart to open. This is the best way to open and receive energy.	*1. The Heart Communicates, focus on receiving -* Your partner is appreciating you. Notice everything your heart feels. Allow yourself to feel things you may never have felt before. Open up and allow the love from your partner to silently speak. They will enjoy the loving and tender appreciation your heart holds for them. It nourishes and heals you both. The most common response is "I love you, I love you, I love you!" Let yourself feel love for your partner, and allow their love in.
2. Focus on receiving from her heart - You are receiving energy into your chest. Focus on the appreciation for all you give. This requires no words. Allow yourself to be adored, and open your heart. If visualization helps, try imagining a golden river filling your ocean; silver or gold sparkles or electricity	*2. Energy Flow –* Imagine the heart center in the middle of your chest is exuding love into your partner. Think about how good it feels and how much you appreciate their arms around you. Imagine that you are flowing a stream of sparkles into their chest. Add to the energy flow if you like, by

flowing into you. Make up something that brings the most pleasure.	using images. Think about your heart's emotions as a river flowing into their ocean. You may see the warmth of your heart fire flowing in and comfortably burning inside of their hearth.
3. Hold her tight enough - Use your strength so your receiving partner can feel your intent to create a safe and secure space in your arms. Practice with different pressures to see how they respond most favorably. My favorite is a very strong bear hug sort of pull, but some receivers prefer a softer embrace. Use common sense, and make sure it feels good to your partner.	*3. Trust him to hold you* - Drop everything and know he's GOT YOU. You are safe to let go of worry and be held. Allow him to support you and take deep breaths, identifying any tension in your body, and letting it out with a sigh. Notice any resistance and let that go too.
4. Let Go/Focus – Relax your mind and focus all of your attention on your heart center in the middle of your chest. Let go of thoughts, worries, fears, and feel your heart receiving your partner's energy. This sensation is not always clear for givers as they begin this practice. It seems paradoxical	*4. Focus on Pleasure* – Tune in to how you feel. If you can feel the energy flowing, ask your partner to adjust slightly to see if you can feel it more intensely. Experiment. This is how you become more tuned into the flow between you. Feel the pleasure deeply! Don't be afraid to speak up and ask him

to hold and give while still opening and receiving. *Do not worry about this at all, just be in the moment, breathe more deeply and focus on feeling.* Notice the amazing effect it has on your partner. Once you both relax into the embrace and allow the flow, you will notice your pleasure increasing.

to adjust. Know his desire is to take care of you. It is what sets you free to have the best sex – or no sex, or whatever feels right to you, every single time! Notice trust, and tenderness. Let yourself be amazed and feel as if you are "flying to the moon" or even tapping into eternity!

5. Be still, then move gently - Relax and be still. Resist the urge to rock or sway yet as this can interrupt the focus on the electrical current. Breathe deeply while your partner feels you. Imagine the plug of your hand like a cord stuck in an electrical outlet and see it as a conduit for energy. After a few minutes, you may rock just slightly, very slowly, while supporting them with your strength. If your partner resists movement, go back to stillness until they are ready to move with you.

5. Allow sounds of healing and move with it - it is natural to make sounds of deep contentment such as purring or moaning. You may become aware of layers of a lifetime of sadness peeling away from your heart. You have moved into a flow state where your pleasure takes over. Allow yourself to move with it. Be in the moment. Listen to your body, and pay attention to your partner. This is where you are present to the honesty and sensual pleasures that will be your guiding force.

6. Notice responses – Watch for these signals that you have successfully pulled your

6. Body Signals – There are many signals that indicate you have been received into the

partner's heart energy into yours. *Shift of mood* - Relaxes and let go of stress, lets out a big sigh. *Soft kisses* - You begin to receive kissing your neck or even light nibbles. You feel her desire. *The "rag doll effect"* - Your partner drops in your arms – this is the sign of surrender to your embrace. You will be more likely to feel heart energy flowing into your heart as your partner's sensual Divine Feminine energy is open and moving. Remember to maintain your hold. *Tenderness* – You can feel the love, sweetness and tenderness in your loving embrace. This is meant for you. Enjoy it! *Arousal* - After some practice, you may feel as if you are actually inside of her when she pulls your energy in.	heart center. Notice if you feel any of these. Pay attention to your own personal signals. ~ A natural desire to shift deeper into their arms ~ Wanting to kiss or nibble their neck ~ Smiling from ear to ear ~ Breathing relaxes, and deep sighs ~ Talking ceases, nervousness disappears ~ Feeling warmth rising in your bodies ~ Not wanting the feeling to end ~ Vibrations may pulse up the center from your genitals into your heart ~ Feeling loved, adored, appreciated, honored and respected ~ Feeling secure and trusting ~ Noticing heat or tingling in the genitals
7. Let nature do its thing - An erection or desire for sex is quite normal when this energy flows. It means you are	*7. Let nature do its thing* - A feeling of sexual desire, or heat in the genitals is quite normal when this energy flows. It

healthy! Pay attention to how your partner responds. Let the intensity of arousal rise and fall for a while.	means you are healthy! Pay attention to how your partner responds.
8. *Tenderness embrace* – This is an important variation of The Power Embrace. Place the palm of your dominant hand on the back of her neck and pull your partner *gently* into you. Make sure the non-dominant hand is on target with the back of the heart center. This is the next level of trust and surrender and she may become completely limp, like a ragdoll in your arms.	8. *Dropping like a ragdoll* - This is a clear and important indicator to your partner that the energy in your heart has fully released into his. It can be likened to the energy release he has in his genitals with an orgasm. Allow yourself to be held and supported. You have entered *the feminine receptive mode,* a deliciously tender space of trust. It signals the masculine to be in control and support you in your feminine power.

Notes for both:

Experimenting - As you practice, you will naturally experiment with hand placement on different parts of the back. The entire upper back and upper chest is the heart center zone. Notice which energy centers (1-7) give different responses. Moving the hands up

and down the back to sense the strongest connection which ignites your sexual desire. Keep a solid connection on the heart target to bring best results while you move the other.

Trust the Process - Remember, many people have been starved for intimate attention. This experience may be entirely new. Begin with the intention of releasing all stress and allowing yourself to relax and "fall in love" with your partner. Remember that the feeling of love happens in the moment as the energy of appreciation is exchanged.

Fill your partner's bucket - Some have not had their heart touched this way for decades. If your partner's emotional bank account is in the red, you may need to "fill their bucket" for a while.

Stick with it. - Spend the time allowing the loving feelings to flow until you both feel satisfied. It may take minutes, days or weeks.. Be the space for this healing. Be a warm hearth to rest by. Remember that though this is written as men holding women, you can try reversing it so the woman takes on the role of loving and supporting her man.

Let the bucket overflow! - Once the emptiness is filled, the overflow can bring about a desire for sex (if that's what you agree on). It is like giving a starving person a bite of a sandwich. Your partner may be dying for more. Give it to them! Make your partner happy and fill them up. You will most likely be beautifully rewarded.

Notes on The Power of women's pleasure...

It made sense to me that if we were balancing The Power of the masculine with The Power of the feminine, that they must be equally powerful.

It seemed ridiculous to consider that the female heart energy would be equal to the intense power of the male genitals, but maybe, just maybe, it was true!

It was just a matter of redefining how much attention we put on these organs.

This energy from women will warm and support him with her loving appreciation for all his masculine qualities of strength, courage, providing and protecting, and loving her.

He is able to feel the tenderness that he activates in her as she loves and adores him. It is the nurturing Mother energy that men were taught to shut out long ago in order to achieve manhood and independence.

This comes full circle when he pulls her into his chest as his equal.

She feels ultimate fulfillment when he holds her tightly in appreciation, and it lights up her heart. As a result, it shines on everyone around her. This is a different kind of light only he can inspire. It makes her eyes sparkle and everyone sees it and wants to be like her. They know she is in love.

"Wait - what? You mean I have equal power in my heart to his genitals? When Kari told me this, I opened up and began having so much pleasure between my heart and his, that my boyfriend and I started screaming together (when we knew the neighbors weren't home!) Is this the "heartgasm" I heard of? I think so!"

- Angie, 30

Only he has the keys to unlock the depths of her heart. She counts on him for this, to be the person in her life that appreciates her, loves and honors her for her soft, feminine, emotional and sensual qualities. As he unlocks her heart, she is astounded at how much beauty there is inside. She more easily desires sex with him when she feels this way.

I know I can't resist it. It feels like a fairytale, a dream come true.

Perfumed Garden, 70x100cm, oil on canvas, by Ines Honfi

"I didn't even know the heart-genital energy circuit had been severed in me until Kari showed me the missing link which completed the energy loop. I could never separate my heart from my sexuality again."

- Keith, 64

The connection heals a woman's traumas over time. Just knowing there is at least one man in this world with whom she can be this transparent, honored and accepted for all she is allows her to trust.

Primavera II, 100x100 cm, oil on canvas, mixed technique by Ines Honfi

She can be in her full femininity, loving unconditionally and shining her light brighter and brighter.

If single, like me, a woman can share her heart energy with men knowing how much it heals both. When she allows herself to feel this pleasure fully, it makes the sharing all worthwhile, each and every time. I don't repel men's appreciation and desire for me, but absorb it like the sun's rays, honoring them for their design. My light shines brighter, and I get to be sexually engaged when I choose to.

With the added power of the heart centers during sex, the couple is transformed into the most dynamic and charismatic version of themselves. Love from the feminine transforms the male from animal lust that is seeking sexual release into the most magnificent of creatures. Perhaps he is transformed into a roaring lion, fierce and full of masculine intensity. In the private universe of their making, he becomes confident and secure in his strength as King to please his Queen.

She becomes a more radiant person, floating on clouds while thinking of him. She is fulfilled and happy.

Body Issues Gone! - Instead of a woman feeling empty from lack of attention, or demeaned by disconnected sex, she becomes the most beautiful and tantalizing Goddess when she is appreciated and loved.

She no longer worries if she is overweight or has wrinkles. All of those issues disappear in the perfection she feels inside. She is glowing in radiant love through her heart. Her love added to the equation allows them to access what feels like superpower abilities. The Great Circle of Desire is truly great for a reason. It brings out the very best in us.

"Recognizing the designs of our bodies saved my marriage. I was having unsatisfying sex once a year with my husband when I learned about men's natural design with Kari. I committed to changing my sex life at age 50, and now we have great sex at least twice a month for several hours! This happened nearly 10 years ago and we have kept the fires burning bright. It gets more fulfilling as the years go by."

-Cathy, 59

When love is added to lust, the result is that we are lifted into the best version of ourselves. Our authenticity emerges within the trust we feel. We are free to experiment with our fantasies and explore all our heart's desire. When the heart is included, there is innocence and purity. We become as children playing in the sandbox, full of wonder and curiosity.

The healer revealed - It is time to unlock the mysteries inside of your body, starting with a loving hug.

I invite you to upgrade your belief system, because you too, my friend, have this healing energy inside of you. I'm setting you up for literally the highest form of sex, and it is created through intention.

Once you experience The Great Circle of Desire, you will understand that love itself is the greatest healer.

It is the hidden mystery that is returning to us as our consciousness is evolving and expanding. Don't believe it's possible? I've found it works for everyone who is willing.

Other thoughts:

Does doing this practice mean I am in a "relationship" with the person I have shared with?

Many who hear about such amazing shortcuts to deep intimacy tend to have one of these two very opposite reactions.
- ❖ The feelings are not real.
- ❖ I am in love and this person is my soulmate.

I understand these concerns, so let's get real about this.

The more sensitive my heart became to the effects of The Power Embrace, the more I compared it to drinking a six-pack of beer. I could become "love-drunk", swooning in another blissful world of happiness and joy while merged into a man's heart. Sometimes my smile would be stuck from ear to ear and I couldn't stop it. (Who would do that?)

You can see why this hug is so very powerful!

This is a "high" that has been missing from humanity, that people search out with drugs and alcohol. Most of us believe we must be in a committed relationship to feel this way - relaxed, free, open, and loved. Yet I found it available in everyone who is willing to try it. We are designed for this fulfillment.

Each person will have to be responsible for choosing what type of relationship is desired and standing for it. This heart connection is very beautiful and very powerful. Women will feel like they are in love, and men will feel appreciation, arousal and desire for sex.

When you can be open and in this flow of connection and pleasure, your energy is incredibly powerful, and exudes such a high vibration, it will change your entire reality and uplift everyone you touch. Ultimately, it changes the world. Making good choices on how to use that energy is your responsibility, always. Women may not want to continue into a sexual space, and at first men might not understand that when they feel so loved and appreciated.

Use this energy and knowledge wisely. It is great only if it serves the purposes and honors the boundaries that work for *both partners*. In your integrity, you would never take advantage of someone who has had too much to drink, so respect that your partner might need clear communication before making decisions about having sex when they are "love-drunk".

If you don't know how to communicate at a level where you can ask for what you want, say yes, or no, and change your mind in the moment, you might consider taking time to explore that. You can enjoy all of this while maintaining your power.

Short-term "in the moment" - To be completely present with someone who is in front of you, as they are, with complete respect, is a powerful thing. It is completely possible to be deeply connected and flowing with someone short term. It requires that you both be free of expectations and any attachment to long-term commitment.

As a single person, The result is that I could have a beautiful experience with a man, that was close and fulfilling, and avoid any cold-heartedness. This allowed me to expand my sexuality and learn about sexual ecstasy.

Depending on the awareness of partners, this beautiful connection holds potential benefits of juicy explorations, trauma healing, and profound intimacy – without strings attached or expectation.

Long-term - "partnered" If you have decided to only have long-term committed relationships, then by all means, use The Power Embrace to establish and deepen the intimacy you feel with another. Once your couple-ness is established to your liking, The Power Embrace will keep you connected for as long as you use it, taking you deeper and deeper into the heartspace.

Continually opening you to greater erotic experiences, the benefit to committed couples is expressed in creating long-term, sustained intimacy that grows stronger with each embrace. Couples have the added benefit of building their foundation of love stronger with each passing day.

No matter what relationship style you choose to experience, the skill and sensitivity level increases over time. Focus on your own experience, and notice what you need to work on to be more flowing with each interaction.

It is gorgeous any way you slice it. You can't lose because connection makes sex a more soulful endeavor that celebrates all of the beauty of being human. Take the time to honor yourself and your boundaries, to create the deepest and most satisfying experiences.

Loving you, 100x100 cm, oil on canvas, by Ines Honfi

"It took us several tries before we really felt the subtle energies that created the circle of desire. After that, we began feeling things all over our bodies we never knew were possible! We plan to do this every day for the rest of our lives."

- Scott and Emily, Seattle

"Over many years of practicing, it was clear that connected, intimate embraces are for everyone. It became the foundation of my work.
After reading through this, you may have feelings come up, questions, or worries. The last part will help you with that, or come get your questions answered in the Facebook Group!

PART ONE - You Want It. You CAN Have It

PART TWO - What it is and How to DO IT

PART THREE - Practices and Challenges

7

Getting to the Starting Point

"Your task is not to seek love, but merely to seek and find all the barriers within yourself that you have built against it."

- Rumi

The point: If you've read this far, and don't know how to approach your partner this chapter is for you! You will learn how to approach the subject using conversation starters as inspirations. It's a good idea to read all of Part Two before starting the conversation.

"I discovered that I could teach my husband how to reach me in the deepest places of my heart. Now, when I want sex, but don't feel ready for it, all I have to do is ask for our special embrace. He knows that I've just handed him the keys to my sexual desire. Everybody wins!" - Jen, 46

Navigating to the space where you can share this practice might take some trial and error. Keep your intention of connecting deeply and be okay with a little awkwardness until you find it.

There are many tips and tricks following to help you find your way into The Great Circle of Desire.

Asking for Appreciation:

This can be initiated by either partner. It may seem quite awkward to ask another person to appreciate you, so here are some ways to start the conversation.

These suggestions will likely feel scripted and awkward. Try saying something like "Can I ask you something that feels awkward?" It can prepare your partner to hear it.

If you find your partner is resistant, let that be okay. Some people aren't ready for this. Look for someone else to practice with, someone you trust. Talk about your own experience with your partner without making it about them.

Conversation starters:

❖ I'm feeling a little awkward bringing this up. I've learned a new technique I'd like to practice for feeling connected with others. It may seem a bit weird, but it is a special hug that is supposed to feel fantastic. Can we try it?

❖ Have you heard about The Great Circle of Desire? It works to connect people's energy centers in the body. I have been wanting to practice this type of hug. Would you be interested in learning? I want to get good at it because it sounds wonderful.

❖ I'm reading about something called The Great Circle of Desire. Have you heard of it? It all begins with a hug, and is supposed to be very relaxing. Would you allow me to try it with you? It might feel weird at first, but I think we can laugh our way through it.

Partners and/or lovers who want to reconnect:

- ❖ I know we have busy lives, and sometimes I feel like I want to just slow down for a moment and be together. I picked up a book and found this practice called a Power Embrace. It is supposed to really relax and recharge us. When would be a good time for us to try it?
- ❖ I've been learning how women want their hearts to be honored as much as men want their cocks appreciated! Who knew? So there's this thing where we both get that at the same time. It's called The Great Circle of Desire. It helps our energies flow together and sounds arousing.
- ❖ Have you heard that women can have heart orgasms? I've been learning about the power men have to open women so they radiate love from their hearts. It actually creates a cycle of energy so men can have orgasms without ejaculating! Would you like to try it? You may not have an orgasm the first time, because it takes practice, but you might!
- ❖ I miss being close to you. A friend told me about something called a Power Embrace. I would really enjoy it if you could pull me tightly into your chest, and appreciate me, while I appreciate you back. Being held would feel really good.
- ❖ Before we have sex the next time, would you try something with me? I just found out about something called The Great Circle of Desire. It sounds weird, but it is supposed to make great sex even better!
- ❖ I may not be in the mood to have sex now, but you can probably change that with a Power Embrace. I found out that when a man wants sex and a woman "just wants to be held", it can actually be a bridge to opening her to want to have sex! Wanna try it?

My wife feels like we have been given a second chance to live like we are on a forever honeymoon! Thank you Kari, for showing us the potential of deep intimacy in sex". - Greg, 68

Talk with your partner about how you feel and what you would like to experience. Find the language that works for you.

Just like anything new, it can be weird the first time. It's okay to laugh, and come back to it. Once you have had the conversation and found a partner, figure out where you will try it.

Remember... Don't overthink it, it's only weird the first time. You will survive the awkwardness!

8

Creating the Space

The point: For best results, find a space that's safe and quiet, or has soft sounds like music, or water flowing. Something pleasant and soothing where you won't be interrupted. Silence the phone.

Common sense would tell us that in order to practice The Great Circle of Desire, and enter a space of flowing energy we need to not be interrupted.

So.

Silence the phone, make sure you don't have anywhere to be, and take care of your physical and mental needs FIRST.

Use the bathroom, have a glass of water, or snack.

Side note: Your mental state can be greatly shifted during this practice, so you can try it if you are feeling a little tired, as long as your "giver" partner has agreed to support you.

Environment:

Indoors works fine. Find a place where you will not be interrupted. If you live with people or have kids, shut them out, and tell them you need some quiet time. This is a boundary. If you haven't practiced setting boundaries, now is a good time, but ONLY if they will respect them.

Make sure things feel comfortable. Temperature, lighting, and sounds should be pleasant, or neutral. Music can be really nice.

Being outdoors is WONDERFUL because you can connect to the flow of nature. The same things apply, silence the phone in your pocket if you must bring it. Go away from people, and find a comfortable space when the weather is agreeable.

Mental and emotional space:

Practicing The Great Circle of Desire is like meditation. Give consideration to your mind, mental chatter or thoughts that are present, and time of day. If you are practicing with a partner, talk first to make sure there is nothing that needs to be said that could distract you from being present with the sensual flow.

After you do this practice, you may feel charged up, relaxed or tired. Everyone can respond differently each time. Sometimes emotions may arise that need to flow. You can feel drained and want to rest afterwards if you are new to moving energy this way.

Be gentle and start slow.

During the practice, emotions or thoughts may arise. It is best to take note of them for yourself, and talk about them later, but also okay to let them move through and out with tears, or laughter. Taking deep breaths can help the feelings move more easily.. Sometimes you might not be able to identify the source of the feelings, just know you are healing on deep levels by letting go.

Let your partner have their experience and don't make it about you. For best results, commit to the practice regularly! Just like any exercise, the more we do it, the better we get.

"We made an agreement with each other to feel this intimacy every day of our lives like Kari suggested and it just keeps getting better! We have such trust and closeness now that we both can be fun and creative and sexy without embarrassment. Sex often follows naturally, and we are free to be ourselves!"

- James, 45, Seattle

A Space For Sex

It's nice to be in a space where you can have sex after this practice if you desire to. Set it up with that intention if you and your partner are using the practice to have better sex!

Making plans in advance and other amazing practices

Opposite of what we have been told, anticipation is the best aphrodisiac. Always plan the next time you will be together and prepare for it with creative sexy ideas.

Partners have come up with creative ways to communicate their desires to each other while waiting for their playdates to arrive. I have found a few favorites. They are like a private language of love codes between partners.

❖ *The Coupon book* – Marriages have been saved with the coupon book. Design a coupon book with some cut and stapled paper. Offer things your partner loves and can't resist to get the ball rolling. Ask for a 24-hour notice so you can have fun preparing for the activity.

❖ *The Candy Dish* – Keep a candy jar with mixed hard candies. Assign a meaning to each one to represent your sexual delights. Place the candies in your special dish to indicate what you're in the mood for and watch for your lover to respond with a favorite candy in the dish.

❖ *Monopoly Money* – Make an agreement to pay for your pleasures. Allot each other an amount of play money and decide together on the value of each service. Earn the money from the other for your more expensive pleasures.

❖ *Barometer of Desire* – Design a paper thermometer for the fridge with a magnet that can be moved up and down the temperature gauge. This will tell your partner how hot and ready you are. Or maybe it should be placed in a more private place…

❖ *Weekly Escape Playdates* – Plan at least 2-4 hours of fun and frolic with your partner. Make sure you are uninterrupted and have time to relax, play and explore in a leisurely manner.

❖ *Monthly Staycation* – Plan a mini getaway that is like a honeymoon. Get a sitter for the kids. Go to a hotel if you can. Spend time focusing on each other. Talk and listen. Bring up the things that have been set aside while life keeps happening. Make promises to expand your love. Speak your wedding vows again.

❖ *Learn to massage each other* - Buy a massage table. I call this the next best thing after The Power Embrace, to relax your partner and have the best sex ever! Massage helps to quiet the mind and open the body for pleasure. You will learn new ways to explore your partner. Ask how they like to be touched, and practice getting into the flow of erotic energy. Pleasure heals! Watch some videos or take some classes. This is a great way to keep growing closer for life. Always have spa necessities on hand and ready such as massage oil, towels, music and candles. Prepare the room to be as close to a beautiful spa as possible and get creative.

❖ *The Speed of Love* - Most of us know how to move at a standard speed or get excited and very intense. There is another way that is sure to bring wonder to your senses.

Slow down. And then, slow down some more. Think snail's pace.

With trillions of cells in the body, each one containing ½ watt of electricity, they each have the capacity to orgasm! It is called a goosebump, but should be called a cell-gasm. It takes a very slow movement for the cells to pick up a sensation and carry it to the brain and create a response back to the sender. Moving this slowly requires determination and focus. It is easy to move quickly and miss the trillions of cells that sing their delights when you pay attention at that level.

When you match the speed of cellular communication, you know it. You feel far more when you tap into "the zone". It is very sensual and erotic, as you are now making love with every cell in your partner's body. Vary your timing and notice the difference it makes.

❖ *Intentional breathing* - Face each other in an embrace, foreheads touching. Synchronize your breath until it feels natural, then reverse it so one is inhaling when the other is exhaling. When he exhales, he should visualize pushing his energy down with his breath, and out of his penis, penetrating her, filling her with love and power while she is inhaling and pulling it all up into her vagina and even further up into her heart. This is a powerful practice! When she exhales, she should push love out of her breasts into his chest while he opens his heart to receive it. Make sounds, sigh, moan, groan, roar on each exhale to intensify the energy. Don't fight the urge to move with it. Notice your attraction and desire arise!

❖ *Penis of Love* - Sound corny? You won't think so once you try this one! Another version of slowing down, a woman can be driven out of her mind in ecstasy when the man uses his intention to love the woman through his penis! Just like focusing his appreciation of her into his heart and pulling her in, he can use this same power to love her through penetration.

For men, simply imagine that you are your penis. That's right! It's just the opposite of what you have been told all your life. Now, imagine that your head is now the head of your penis. Your body is the shaft. You will be in your favorite playground of pleasure, head first!

Enter her vagina at a snail's pace. You are now an explorer, going head-first into the mystery of the woman. It will take you at least one to five full minutes to enter fully, so prepare to breathe deeply through it.

Women often accumulate sore spots inside their vaginas, just from day-to-day stress. One day sex feels great, and the next day is hurts. Those sore spots are your opportunity to massage her with love and bring her back to health and well-being.

Ask her to tell you if there is a sore spot so you can gently massage it with the head of your penis. It will feel super-good to you as it alleviates her pain. It is your positive charge balancing her negative charge. Once the pain has subsided, move slowly to the next. Focus on all the pleasure you feel in doing so. Keep gently massaging her sore spots until there are none left.

At this point, she will be experiencing crazy love for your penis! Her vagina will feel very free and open, begging you for more. You may also use your fingers or toys or whatever she desires.

Men who can do this are worth their weight in gold, and it is only a matter of patience until they start feeling the pleasure. Then it is not work, but ecstasy! When men do it with me, even the beginners on their very first time often end up in such pleasure that they begin moaning loudly and climaxing before fully inside.

A man can imagine that the walls of her vagina are hugging and squeezing him, saying to his penis, "He's here! Love has arrived!"

Tell all the cells and muscles that you are here to bring great pleasure and healing and ask them to squeeze you more tightly than ever and orgasm all over you. Keep practicing putting your full focus on this and you will be amazed!

Imagine the energy from your penis extends clear up to her heart. The fully attentive love from the penis will complete The Great Circle of Desire in the most powerful way possible!

9

Troubleshooting

The point: Some will find this practice easy and natural, and some may have obstacles. This chapter deals with things like broken hearts, ego trips, and trauma. The key is to gain more understanding, and keep going at the pace that you need.

Frustration or fear of the process of finding true intimacy can come from several places, but don't despair! It's all okay, you can work through it if you are willing! Mastering the process takes practice, so listen to your inner guidance. Also be aware that if one or both partners have emotional or mental health issues, they may not allow this connection. If it seems impossible, seek professional counsel.

Block #1 - The broken heart

After a relationship that was painful, reconnecting can be very scary. It is common and natural to hide and protect our hearts when we have not properly healed from past pain.

If you know this is an issue for you, it can be hard to talk about it. Both men and women can have this experience. If you encounter it, the greatest gift you can give your partner is communication and taking it slow.

If you haven't allowed enough time and healing after the previous relationship, trying to force connection may not work well either.

Both can benefit from deeper communication about this.

If the broken heart is yours, try these words:

- ❖ "I am aware that my past hurt is coming up right now, and I would appreciate your help in healing it. Are you willing to hold me so I can work through this and feel safe?"
- ❖ "I know we just met and I want to be able to be vulnerable with you. It isn't your fault, but I feel unsure now because I have had some painful experiences. Can you hold me while I sort through this?"
- ❖ "I'm finding that talking about doing this practice is bringing up feelings of tension, and I'm not ready yet. Can you hold my hands and sit with me while I explore what I'm feeling and why I'm resisting it?"

If you notice your partner seems to be hurting, try these words:

- ❖ "I would love to be able to share this intimacy with you, but I feel like we should go slow. Your comfort is important to me."
- ❖ "I am feeling like there is something causing resistance, and that's okay, I don't want to push it. Do you want to talk about it?"
- ❖ "Can we go a little slower and just hold hands first? I want to establish a safe space, and I care about you. As much as I want to jump into a full embrace, let's just be present in this way first."

The benefits of taking the time to listen and see your partner greatly outweigh rushing into an embrace that isn't connected. Remember, there could be a learning curve, but when you face your resistances and fears, and allow someone to hold you through it, you will heal from past traumas and pain. Work together without judging yourself or your partner. Go back to a "first date" scenario, have coffee or tea together, and get to know each other again.

"Kari knows what she's talking about! I used this information with the women I was dating, and they felt the difference instantly. One even said she only felt that kind of closeness with her ex-husband during their honeymoon and never thought she would find it again!"

- Chad, 44

Also remember that if it simply isn't working, you might need a different partner to practice with, or other methods to connect.

Block #2 - The ego trip

Some people are shut down, and not ready, willing or able to be vulnerable. Working with these people can be very difficult, so be aware and honest whether the person is a good partner for you.

Let's say you approach your husband, who you haven't been intimate with for years, or maybe you have sex, but it's the disconnected kind. This is a challenging space to break open, and trying to initiate The Great Circle of Desire may not be a successful first step.

They may say something like:
- ❖ "I just don't like that."
- ❖ "Why would I want to do that? Our sex life is fine."
- ❖ "Sounds weird, no thanks."

When you meet this strong resistance, you can back down, or you can be gently persistent.

Remember that you deserve a loving connected relationship, so if you feel confident that you can crack through the resistance, try these words:

- ❖ "I miss being close to you, and I would really like to explore this to reconnect."
- ❖ "I feel like we both want a sex life again, but don't know how to reconnect. Can we find time to talk about this?"
- ❖ "One of my friends told me that this worked for her and her husband and they are so happy again. I miss you. I want that with you, I want the man I married back. I miss being close to you."

Relationships are complicated, so this of course, can't replace couples therapy unless you are both willing to give it a try. Talking to a close friend and role playing the conversation with your partner can increase the comfort level.

Block #3 - The uneducated or inexperienced

"Why weren't we taught this basic principle in sex-ed 101? It would have saved a lot of trouble for all of us." - Jon, 22

Most people learn about basic anatomy and sexual function among nervous peers in our preteen years...

Sometimes people don't learn much more.

They just don't know that vulnerability, appreciation and connection are a thing!

At what point in our childhood do we learn to appreciate and connect with each other?

Our models for relationships are typically our parents. If they model a loving and connected relationship, we learn by watching and seeing it as normal. We are often better at all this vulnerability stuff when we have solid role models.

I mean, obviously, right?

But how many of us grew up in an environment of suppression, guilt and shame around sensuality?

One of the biggest blocks is when we simply don't know what we don't know. Remember that even if you do have this foundation, your partner may not.

Sex Ed is taught, clinically, then usually reinforced with fear based messages of STDs and reasons not to have sex. That's been the typical system.

The desire to learn about sexuality is natural, but how many young people turned to the most accessible source, pornography... and never turned back?

Where are the resources we need to learn about healthy expressions of love and affection? We live in a time when these resources are finally becoming available.

More parents are raising kids in a "sex positive" culture and empowering them with knowledge to take care of themselves and establish boundaries before sharing their body with someone.

During the past 10 years, I have been repeatedly blown away as I learned more and more about what I didn't know I didn't know. I am always open to learning, and I love sharing my discoveries.

I hope you will join the conversation in the Facebook Group, and empower yourself with education, no matter your age!

Block #4 - This feels weird - alternative positions

The Great Circle of Desire practice is described as a standing practice because it's easiest to align hands and bodies and get the concept across.

It may not be ideal for everyone to stand for it, especially for longer sessions. This practice can be done in a modified way to accommodate any physical limitations, size differences, or health limits.

Give these a try:

- ❖ **Sitting facing each other.** Hold hands, breathe together, touch knees if you can, and look into each other's eyes while breathing deeply. The energy may not be as easy to feel, but it can still flow this way. If it feels weird, talk about it, or take turns acknowledging each other.
- ◆ **Spooning cuddle.** Giver holds receiver, laying behind them on a comfortable bed or couch. Hold hands, or "plug in" (put hands on your partner) where it feels comfortable. The connection will be felt in this position because energies flow from front and back of our bodies. You may already have experienced this feeling that spooning creates!

Remember the energy flows from front and back of both bodies, so you can switch who is the "big spoon" and "little spoon". Most men really enjoy the nurturing feeling of their woman snuggling up from behind!

❖ **Hugging Cuddle.** Same as standing, but situate your bodies in a laying down position, facing each other. This can be any cuddle position that allows you both to fully relax without losing circulation. Remember to keep hands on each other to increase energy flow.

The connection can be made in many ways, just set the intention to share it and open the flow! Stay present! Keep your thoughts focused on the person you are with.

Block #5 - Self Care and Awareness

If you are struggling with this, be honest about how you feel right now, in your life, in your body, in your relationship, or lack thereof.

❖ Set an intention that you are willing to be more vulnerable, open, or trusting, and ask for the appropriate partner to show up in your meditation or prayers.

❖ If you think you want sex, take a moment to see if that's what will serve your highest purpose right now. Sometimes, we can use sex as a distraction when we are scared to be vulnerable and shut down the healing intimacy that's available.

❖ Be aware of your past pain and honor it. This practice can heal your heart and allow you to open and trust again, but be sure it's time.

❖ If you begin to fantasize about something that is not happening in the moment, bring yourself back to the present feelings and sensations. The energy that feels so good is easy to use to fuel fantasies, so instead of drifting away, flow that energy back into your partner in the moment. If you like, tell your partner about your fantasy and ask them to share too. Place a hand on their heart or go back to The Power Embrace to return to the connection.

Block #6 - I DON'T HAVE A PARTNER!!!!!

Here's how to do this practice all alone. It is actually a variation of masturbation, or as I prefer to say, *self-pleasuring* meditation, (or simply, selfing!) but without the direct stimulation to the genitals.

If you can't tune into this subtle energy easily, try awakening your body with movement or genital self-pleasuring first. Then the energy will be more tangible and you can be present with the more subtle feelings.

When circulating energy by yourself you will understand and feel the sensations. When you find a partner to share with you will be confident and teach them to share it with you!

❖ Lay on your back, on a comfortable surface
❖ Close your eyes and take a few deep breaths
❖ Take a few more deep breaths allowing your belly to expand

- ❖ Just as you would place your hands on your partner, place them on yourself.
  - ➤ For men - Place dominant hand on the heart and the non dominant hand on, or just above the penis. This allows the energy to flow out of the penis, through the arms, and back into the heart, back down the spine to the penis, creating a circuit.
  - ➤ For women - Place dominant hand on the vulva, and the non dominant hand on heart. This creates a circuit from the heart down to the genitals, which flows up the spine and back out the heart.
- ❖ Visualize the flow of energy through the circuit.
- ❖ Breathe with the energy.
  - ➤ For men - Inhale and pull energy from your heart down your spine, then exhale and release it from your penis into your non dominant hand. This is a flow of energy, not an ejaculation. An erection may happen and increasing pressure on it may feel good while you continue breathing. Feeling good is okay!
  - ➤ For women - Inhale and pull energy into your vagina and up your spine then exhale and feel it release from your chest, breasts, and heart. After some time practicing, you may feel as if you are being physically penetrated. It's pretty amazing.
- ❖ Breathe deeply, and allow sound on the exhale. The vibrations will increase pleasurable sensations. Let it go, moan, sigh, growl, scream or whatever you feel!
- ❖ Continue to breathe deeply and circulate the energy. As you continue, emotions may arise. Let them out! It will feel weird at first! GO WITH IT! Cry, laugh, scream, growl.
- ❖ As you build this energy, you may begin to tremble or undulate as the energy flows through your body. Don't judge it, let it flow! Surrender to your body's responses.

- ❖ Change up the speed and duration of your breaths to match the sensations, faster, slower, quieter, louder, explore what feels good to you!
- ❖ Continue the practice until you feel complete. Depending on how much energy you have moved, this can be many things, and all of them are okay!
  - ➢ Tingly and warm all over
  - ➢ Desiring orgasm, and wanting to masturbate
  - ➢ Peaceful
  - ➢ Hungry
  - ➢ Sleepy

Though it is nice to have a partner, when you learn this alone it is incredibly satisfying to use the practice to energize yourself any time.

For men, when you learn to circulate energy this way you will be able to have sex longer and even have orgasms without ejaculaton! Masturbation/self-pleasure becomes a recharging and release that contributes to your vitality and stamina.

For women, don't let your sexual appetite die between partners. This practice keeps things from becoming stagnant, and also contributes to overall health and vitality.

Block #7 - PORN.

Thank you to one of our Facebook group members for this VERY VALUABLE scenario. This is a common problem. Let's look at ways to address it:

"My partner likes porn. I don't mind that he watches it, I just don't want to be part of his porn experience. He's better at sex than love. He's competent in one and has been hurt in the other. His defense is to make fun of stuff or brush it off. I trust him in a lot of ways, but I don't know how to approach this technique without his laughing at it."

First of all, thank you for submitting this feedback as we were wrapping up the book! There are a few things going on here that might make The Great Circle of Desire almost impossible to initiate with him.

- ❖ *"Not wanting to be part of his experience."* This is likely from the feeling of detachment instead of connection, so let's let that be what it is for the moment. If he is watching porn to his completion, and not leaving any energy for you, it might be a good idea to explore how your relationship IS working well, and focus on that.
  - ➢ Is the good stuff good enough?
  - ➢ Write a gratitude list from your perspective.
- ❖ *"He has been hurt in love, and is defensive or avoiding intimacy."* This is a place where you can work on your own expression of love without him.
  - ➢ Is he interested in seeing you as the beautiful expression of love and sensuality that you are?
  - ➢ Do you get a "wow" when you walk into the room?
  - ➢ Do you feel turned on around him at all?
- ❖ Here are some ideas:
  - ➢ Be aware of how you are showing up, and if he isn't interested, examine that. If you have slipped into couch potato mode and wear nothing but pajamas and don't take care of yourself, that may cause issues.
  - ➢ Look in the mirror and ask yourself if you would want to be with you. Are you happy? Smiling? Radiant? You deserve to be with someone who sees you, loves you, and wants to devour you. If you don't FEEL sexy and desirable, spend some time on that, for you.
  - ➢ Find something to watch that is arousing to you, erotic, or romantic, and let yourself feel into your own sensuality. What turns you on? Has he seen you turned on recently?

➢ Wear something that makes you feel sexy and beautiful. Take time for self nurturing when he is watching porn. Whether it's a warm bath, or self-pleasuring, find something you can enjoy.

➢ Be a Great Circle of Desire Ninja… Don't tell him what it is, just keep it simple and set an intention in your own mind to connect deeply with him. Instead of explaining, just ask him to hold you. Imagine the energy flowing between you. Does he have the capacity to be present with you?

➢ See if you can get the energy moving by yourself. It can take some patience, but when you are warmed up, and flowing alone, it is more likely that he will fall into the flow with you.

➢ Include him in your mind's eye, and visualize him doing exactly what you desire, and saying exactly what you want to hear. Remember that our perception of people is a big part of how we see them, so find all the things you love about him, and imagine the rest, see if he steps into a new vibration!

➢ Get real. Sometimes we are in a relationship that simply isn't aligned anymore, and we kick and scream to stay in it. If that's the case, get real.

➢ Ask a friend to be really honest about how they see your relationship.

➢ Step outside and watch yourself with your partner, and ask yourself if you are living the highest expression of joy that you can.

➢ Never stay in an abusive relationship. Abuse and neglect are not ingredients in a good relationship. Learn from it, and get out of it.

If you find yourself still struggling after these troubleshooting tips, consider that there might be something else that needs attention first. Have you talked to someone about how you feel? Remember to be gentle with yourself, these practices can be quite life changing, so come back when you feel more ready.

Find a trusted friend, coach, or counselor to talk with and see what is revealed. Take care of yourself, you deserve to feel amazing!

Floating in serenity, 100x100 cm, oil on canvas, by Ines Honfi

Conclusion

By design, The Great Circle of Desire guides us back to the love, pleasure, and fulfillment of our deepest needs for connection and appreciation. Starting with The Power Embrace, hearts activate the missing link that completes the pathway to intimate and erotic fulfillment, super-charging aliveness, and returning us to the long lost Garden of Eden. In essence, we enter "The Erotic Now".

Hints of eternity and our divine origins become apparent, right there, in the magical embrace of each other. With so much pleasure, we become present, fully embodied, natural human beings connected to our highest and truest, most content and happiest selves. By touching the divine within we find that life here on earth can be the enriching wonderland we once believed possible.

We are designed for returning to this expansion of love with each other at this very special time in our history. Humanity is becoming aware now that we are creating a new beginning in which peace rules while the masculine and feminine love and honor each other in harmony.

Both are, indeed, inside each of us, though our physical forms usually express predominantly as one or the other. As we progress in greater understanding of these natural forces working together, we experience more peace internally and can then offer it externally to others. Armed with information, we can choose our roles authentically, what we like and prefer, rather than have them choose us. There is more space for everyone to make empowering choices.

Everyone can relax and be themselves.

Once you practice The Great Circle of Desire, you know it is possible! You now have a basic introduction to the awakening and balancing of masculine and feminine energies.

 I hope you have enjoyed this little journey into the possibility of a more pleasurable and ecstatic life, one long blissful hug at a time!

"When women give men what has been missing, men will end the wars in this world"

- Cosmic Kari Star

The path of love III, 100x120 cm, oil on canvas, by Ines Honfi

Afterword
by Andrea Nicole King

Hey friends, it's Andrea again. What a great experience working with Kari on this book has been! There are several reasons.

First of all, I know it was time to share this because it was so EASY!

After pondering how to share this information I was watching a movie, National Treasure, and I got it.

At the end of the movie Nicholas Cage's character, John Adams Gates, finds the trigger to open the door to an immense amount of riches.

He had said, "The knights who found the vaults believed that the treasure was too great for any *one* man, not even a king."

When the vaults are opened and he actually sees the treasure, we know the right person has found it. He contacts authorities to distribute, share, and display the wealth across the world.

This is how I feel about Kari's treasure trove of experiences. We all have beautiful gifts inside of us to share. It is a vault of information, wisdom and experiences that can benefit others. Sometimes it stays hidden for a long time.

When Kari asked me to help her share her message, and do the work Spirit has guided her to do, I knew I could be a bridge between her work and her audience.

Just like the treasure room, we will share this wisdom a little at a time, so you can integrate and embody it. We know that information isn't helpful unless you can put it into practice, and it is our goal to share enough to give you an experience, but not so much that it is overwhelming.

We appreciate your feedback and stories!

Before this book, we were working on an exciting trilogy of books which go into much more detail about Cosmic Sex, Connection, and opening into your Divine birthright to ecstasy.

What we realized is that we needed a key to be put in place first. A way to implement the information and embody it. A practice to return to the heart, and connection and appreciation that makes the entire experience of Cosmic Sex possible. The one simple thing that people rush past in most cases.

- ❖ How to be present in the moment.
- ❖ How to feel deeply, using all of our senses.
- ❖ How to observe, feel, and acknowledge someone else's feelings.

This book is that key, and we are honored you have taken the time to read it. Now that you have the key, you will be able to unlock more doors to ecstasy! I hope you have learned a couple of new things, and are excited to expand your Great Circle of Desire Practice.

About the Author

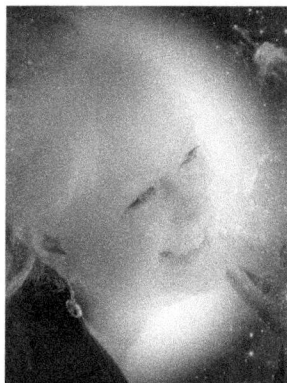

Cosmic Kari's enthusiasm for sharing the keys to ecstasy is exciting and contagious. As an explorer of intimacy, communication, and connection, she has discovered simple ways to reconnect and reach great pleasure.

It is with deep gratitude Kari would like to thank the thousands of people that have learned from her, received her instruction, and helped her to become the teacher and inspirational intimacy coach she is today. Over the past 10 years, these people have been the "Love Lab" testers!

Kari welcomes you to be part of the journey. Expand your ability to experience all of your senses and enjoy your life to the fullest!

About the Cover Artwork

I am an art freak, and I believe in its power to convey messages. I have spent hours in the early mornings searching for sacred sex art online and finding people who create it.

Almost ten years ago, I ambitiously ordered a book cover for my early stories about Cosmic Sex. I discovered George Atherton, a visionary artist and was thrilled when he agreed to create cosmic sex book cover art for me. It was complete in about 3 weeks. What transpired was one of the most well-known and beloved visionary art pieces of sacred sex that has ever been created!

A decade later, with the books finally being published, I needed a new cover, and it had to be as great as George's. I was spoiled. It had to be beautiful. And ancient. After dozens of attempts, and much deliberation, Andrea got a download in the shower. She saw George's image cropped, with an energy circle in the middle of the couple. Easy peasy!

The overlay image Andrea found was a zen "enso", a circular emblem that depicts the creator's unique journey. I got that each person who drew this type of circle, with only one or two swooshes of the paintbrush, would leave a unique imprint that spoke of the nuances of that journey, for others to resonate with while viewing.

Enso (formally spelled ensō) is a sacred symbol in **Zen** Buddhism **meaning circle**, or sometimes, **circle** of togetherness. (How perfect!) The enso is a manifestation of the artist at the moment of creation and the acceptance of our innermost self. It symbolizes strength, elegance, and one-mindedness. The ensō also **symbolizes** absolute **enlightenment**, the universe, and mu (the void).

Did you feel them? The goosebumps? We sure did.

That is pretty deep, but the ensō concept resonated with my desire for the book. After adding a second swipe to the circle, some sparkles, and a few minor adjustments, she showed me the final outcome.

Bingo! The result was magic. The day I saw the cover she created, I was elated all day and knew this was it. Andrea and I are very excited (and proud) when we show the book. Several folks responded, "That is bad-ass!"

We think it's bad-ass too. We're in love with this work and hope you will fall in love with it, too. The image speaks a thousand words.

About Featured Artist Ines Honfi

Ines displays a visionary collection of sensuous romantic Art.
Sensuality and sublime Eros are exhibited together with sophisticated style and refinement.
Being an initiate artist she invites us through her artwork, into a paradisiacal universe where exquisite beauty and intoxicated love merge with elevated passions, leading to spiritual realization and a profound sense of sacredness.

Ines dares to take Erotic Art to another level!

Ines has more than 25 years of experience as an Artist and an Art teacher. In her deep search for inner balance and thirst for knowledge, she found an esoteric school where she learned to alchemize her energies, to awaken her intellect, body, mind, and soul. Afterward, she became as well, a yoga, tantra and meditation teacher on this specific initiate path.
She combines her knowledge of Art and Tantra to transmit her most refined, full of Sublime Eros, visions.

Ines was born in Buenos Aires, Argentina, and she currently lives in Copenhagen, Denmark.

Discover more about her artwork, teachings, and vision at ineshonfi.com
Find her on Instagram and Facebook
Contact: ineshonfi7@gmail.com +45 42229074

Photography Credits

Gratitude for these photographers sharing their works on Unsplash, and Pixabay for use in this work.

Sarandy Westfall, Sergey Nivens, Frank McKenna, Analise Benevides

Catherine Heath, Marcus Dell Col, Krishna Naidu, Wesley Balten

Pablo Heimplatz, Christiana Rivers, Kon Karampelas, Toa Heftiba

Ben White, Alejandra Quiroz, Hannah Reding, Michael Browning

Scott Broome, Brandon Roberts, Jed Villejo

Resources

You made it to the end! Now you have some choices to make.

1. Join the Facebook Group and come chat with other people who are practicing The Great Circle of Desire.
2. Get to it, and practice alone or with a partner.
3. Share this book with a friend.
4. Put this book on the shelf and don't do anything.

I hope you choose anything BUT #4! My passion is to see people opening more and more into their greatest expression of joy and ecstasy. I have so many stories to share, and invite you into the wonderful world of The Great Circle of Desire, and Kari Star's Amazing Adventures in Cosmic Sex! See you there!

-   Cosmic Kari

Facebook Page - https://www.facebook.com/CosmicKariStar/

Facebook Group - https://www.facebook.com/groups/371583417128144/

Website - www.cosmickaristar.com

www.ingramcontent.com/pod-product-compliance
Lightning Source LLC
Chambersburg PA
CBHW021235090426
42740CB00006B/545